THE CRITICAL WRITER

THE CRITICAL WRITER

INQUIRY AND THE WRITING PROCESS

Joyce Armstrong Carroll, EdD, HLD
and Edward E. Wilson

 **LIBRARIES UNLIMITED**

AN IMPRINT OF ABC-CLIO, LLC
Santa Barbara, California • Denver, Colorado • Oxford, England

Library of Congress Cataloging-in-Publication Data

Carroll, Joyce Armstrong, 1937–
  The critical writer : inquiry and the writing process / Joyce Armstrong Carroll, EdD, HLD and Edward E. Wilson.
    pages cm
  Includes bibliographical references and index.
  ISBN 978-1-61069-237-3 (paperback) — ISBN 978-1-61069-238-0 (ebook) 1. Creative writing—Study and teaching.   2. English language—Composition and exercises—Study and teaching.   3. English language—Rhetoric—Study and teaching.   4. Critical thinking—Study and teaching.   5. Inquiry-based learning.   I. Wilson, Edward E.   II. Title.
    PE1404.C345   2014
    808'.042071—dc23   2013050572

ISBN: 978-1-61069-237-3
EISBN: 978-1-61069-238-0

18 17 16 15 14   2 3 4 5

This book is also available on the World Wide Web as an eBook.
Visit www.abc-clio.com for details.

Libraries Unlimited
An Imprint of ABC-CLIO, LLC

ABC-CLIO, LLC
130 Cremona Drive, P.O. Box 1911
Santa Barbara, California 93116-1911

This book is printed on acid-free paper ∞
Manufactured in the United States of America

Dedicated with love forever and hope for her future to Joyce's Goddaughter and namesake Joyce Elizabeth Aldaba—Being a madrina "starts in the soul and goes on for generations." (author unknown)

"Creating Critical Readers, Writers, and Thinkers" resource site

CONTENTS

Contents   **ix**

> The part is always embedded in the whole, the fact is always embedded in multiple contexts, and a subject is always related to many other issues and subjects.
>
> —Caine & Caine

FOREWORD

My good friend's father was a collector and dealer of rare books—often the kind with gilded pages and handsome leather covers. I recall going to his Arizona mountain retreat and seeing shelves and shelves of such books. He frequently tucked into them scholarly reviews and information about the author or the value of the text. When you removed a book from its shelf, both the book and the information he'd gathered awaited the reader. The book you hold is also a rare book—one that recaptures the robust research of the past and couples it with fresh ideas so relevant to the future. It is a book that unfolds in much the same way as the process it aptly describes.

Joyce Armstrong Carroll and Edward E. Wilson, long respected in the field of literacy education, characterize the writer as a discoverer, an inquirer. In doing so, they mirror that very process in both compelling and practical ways for us as teachers. Interweaving brilliant and apt metaphors with robust research, Joyce and Eddie unconceal the process of critical writing through the Carroll/Wilson Schemata—a model not unlike the experience that awaits the reader.

The text is timely; this is the 21st century after all—a time when information is accessible and easy to tap. Teachers must shift readers and writers from passivity to engagement: from recipient to inquirer. The brilliance of Chapter 1 is the way in which the authors illustrate how heuristics fuel discovery and learning. They demonstrate that learners use questions as a mode for participating in the inner conversation of our two selves: the self that makes and the self that evaluates. It is noteworthy that rather than dismiss the role of background knowledge and experiences, they embrace them. Rather than pretending the writer moves from understanding to writing, they suggest just the opposite.

Chapter 2 continues to build on the key ideas introduced in Chapter 1, delving more deeply into the inquiry model. Upon reading the chapter, the reader grows increasingly aware of the "felt sense" of recursiveness in the process of writing and the uniqueness of the writer. I smiled as I read this chapter and thought what pleasure Donald Graves would take in the way the model supports the writer as individual experiences and understandings emerge.

Looking back to look forward is a Carroll-Wilson trademark. It is one of the characteristics I most admire about them as educators and as human beings. Never afraid to recover the rich research of the past, they remind the reader in Chapter 3 of Macrorie's I-Search Paper and the moves the critical writer makes to uncover—to unconceal. Joyce uses the story of Charlie to illustrate the generative power of "searching writing" using their model.

The text would be less complete without the chapter authored by Travis Leech (Chapter 4), an insightful middle school teacher. In this chapter, we gain a bird's eye view of the Carroll/Wilson Inquiry Schemata as it unfolds in a real classroom. The most compelling aspect of this chapter is the perspective of the practitioner. As student writers participate in their own journey of inquiry, the excitement of the teacher is palpable. We "feel" his satisfaction and sense his pride as he sketches the birth and maturation of Mary Beth's essay.

Building on all these ideas, Chapter 5 serves the book as its crescendo. The reader is reminded of Romano's blending of multiple genres. As the authors note, "juxtaposing the known with something similar" opens a door to new understanding and more unconcealment. An artist may add the last brushstroke to the canvas, but the creative process and the joy of discovery is unending. In the same way, the writer continues to find layers of meaning long after the last words are written.

As I close this foreword—a privilege for me to write—I realize I must offer a disclosure. You see I became a Carroll/Wilson student from the moment we met in a writing project classroom in 1988. My teachers are forever learners, which is exactly what makes them the fine teachers they are. They model the very actions they write about and challenge us to do the same. Like a fine meal beautifully served, I enjoyed every morsel of wisdom this text dished up. Classrooms will be livelier places of learning because of this book. Teaching will be more satisfying and joyful. It is a rare book. Delight in it. Cherish it.

Judy Mayne Wallis
EdD in Curriculum and Instruction
Literacy Consultant

REFERENCE

Caine, R. N., and G. Caine. *Making Connections: Teaching and the Human Brain.* California: Innovative Learning Publications (Addison-Wesley Publishing Co.), 1994, 7.

> I write to investigate things I'm curious about.
>
> —Jane Smiley

1 THE CRITICAL WRITER AND WRITING BEHAVIOR

I remember an incident from graduate school when I was assistant director of the Rutgers/Cook Colleges Writing Center. Day after day I sat with students coming into the center with their writing. Some were remedial in the sense that while perhaps brilliant in other academic areas, they struggled with writing—often as a second language. Some just wanted a listening ear. Many in masters or doctoral programs needed, indeed demanded, intense responses, constructive criticism, and detailed suggestions.

I had precious little time to work on my own dissertation. In the evenings I would go home and write and write and write—drivel, lots of drivel before I wrote anything worthwhile. When I met with Dr. Janet Emig, my advisor and mentor, I expressed my exasperation, "Dr. Emig, I am writing and writing but getting nowhere."

She, characteristically reflective, looked me directly in the eye and said, "Why, Joyce, you above all people should know that is your process."

INQUIRY

Grounded in firm theory, this book centers on inquiry, writing as inquiry, inquiry about inquiry, and whatever inquiry yields. Inquiry, like writing, is a process. It occurs in stages, which have been defined differently by different scholars throughout time.

Plato's *inventio,* considered one of the five canons of rhetoric, views it as the process of discovery of arguments. John Dewey divides the process of inquiry into five stages: a felt difficulty, its location and definition, a suggested possible solution, further observation, and acceptance or rejection (Young et al., 77). Young, Becker, and Pike identify four stages: preparation, incubation, illumination, and verification. All agree it's method of discovery and all agree the process is cyclical.

Kenneth Burke's pentad, for example, provides the rhetor with an inquiry guide for students to use when exploring topics. Young, Becker, and Pike call the trigger of inquiry "an uneasiness that grows out of inconsistencies" while they describe the process by which we seek to resolve those inconsistencies as "the movement from this feeling of uneasiness to some adequate solution" (73). The uneasiness may be a student's grappling with a topic, unknowns such as rotten seeds, the fragility of life, or how the Caribbean school system affects lives.

In this book, we hold that inquiry is the hinge that junctures critical thinking with critical writing. We further hold that the stage of illumination holds the key to all good critical writing as it is then that the mind makes that imaginative leap, that Eureka! from some subconscious activity to conscious knowing. That is the moment of unconcealment.

UNCONCEALMENT

The Critical Writer also presents practical strategies to help students become "discoverers," critical writers in various genres. These strategies help students unconceal the truth of what they are saying and in doing so help their writing achieve depth and breadth, be more substantive, and tap their "felt sense" while resolving this feeling of uneasiness. We use the Carroll/Wilson Inquiry Schemata as guide and model.

All too often students think of the act of putting a word down and following it with another and another as tantamount to hammering into stone. Once done, it is finished never to be touched again. Yet the act of writing is the process of uncovering and discovering, the teasing out of authentic meaning.

The famous optical illusion called "Rubin's Vase" features two dark silhouetted profiles facing each other with space or a white "vase" between them. At first glance the picture looks like a glob of white in the middle of a dark background. Yet, if a person looks at the white space, a vase emerges; if a person looks at the dark space, the profiles emerge. The point here is it is impossible to see both at the same time. So, too, students who write without a schema, without process, who fail to read what they have written, fail to read it again and again look at only this aspect of their writing or that aspect. These writers will never enter into the act of unconcealment, never get at the truth of what they want to say. They can achieve true meaning only by becoming a critical writer.

The goal of writing invites participation in unconcealment, bringing something to cognitive awareness. Heidegger captured it in this brief dialogue:

JAPANESE: One says: you have changed your standpoint.
INQUIRER: I left an earlier standpoint, not in order to exchange it for another, but rather because even the prior position was merely a stopover while underway. What is enduring in thinking is the way. (Wrathall, 5)

This exchange encapsulates our philosophy of critical writers. Their task is to keep a constant and consistent process of thinking underway. This means writers craft ways to say what they want to say, keeping those that work but abandoning those that do not, thereby setting out on a different tack, using different words, modifying the syntax, adding, subtracting, rearranging, or even scrapping the entire attempt. In that way writers actively participate in unconcealment, as they bring to the surface of their awareness (and to their papers) deeper and deeper insights. What rises up from that process becomes more truthful and more worthy to share with others.

THE WORD *CRITICAL*

Thanks to the inventive Anglo-Saxons coupled with the many invasions of Britain (not to mention the influence of Shakespeare), contemporary English shows a penchant for multi-meaning words. *Critical* is one such word.

Most of the time when we hear *critical,* we think of criticism—helpful or unfavorable commentary. Sometimes we think *critical* connotes an emergency or urgency. But as is the case with so many words in the English language, the meaning of *critical* depends upon context.

So to be clear, in this text we apply *critical* in its etymological sense. Coming to us from the Latin *criticus* and the Greek *kritikos,* we use *critical* to mean "able to discern or judge," that is, the student author's ability to discern and judge by making sense *of* and *in* his or her writing. In that sense, *critical* provides the foundation for the sound research and rich pedagogy in this book.

FELT SENSE

Our use of *critical* in the term "critical writer" embraces the meaning generated by Eugene Gendlin who speaks of "felt apperception," the mental processes people employ to make sense of a new idea by assimilating and accommodating it (to use Piaget's terms) into their personal world of experiences.

Sondra Perl, building upon the work of Grendlin, calls this "felt sense." In Peter Elbow's foreword to Perl's book *Felt Sense,* he further clarifies the meaning of the term first by setting up the usual writing experience where the writer grapples so impatiently with the text that he or she enters into a state of negative frustration. Elbow goes on to explain that "Grendlin and Perl give us guidance in learning to attend to that felt nonverbal sense" by *honoring* the offending text through a *dwelling in the experience* that causes the frustration. This dwelling often provides "a string to the feeling of what we *are* trying to say—our *felt sense* of meaning" (Perl, v).

In other words, the meaning hides; it is concealed. Not unlike the message in the poem titled "A Valentine for Ernest Mann" by

Naomi Shihab Nye, where Nye, upon describing a valentine of two skunks, talks about the poems hiding in the eyes of those skunks—the beauty of it (Carroll & Wilson, P.A.L., 16). So often the writer's task is not to simply state meaning but to "unconceal" it (to borrow from Martin Heidegger), but that act of unconcealing often makes writing difficult. Students say, "I know what I want to say, but I can't get the words right."

Perl, way ahead of her time, was on to something. This is not just the "stuff" of theory or psychology—it is the way our minds work. Our efficient brains pay attention only to what we perceive as important, or what holds meaning for us. Like the "Rubin's Vase" experience, we only see (understand) what we perceive.

Case in point: For years, we have asked teachers to respond to an experiment adapted from Peter Russell's *The Brain Book*. As they are timed, participants read the brief text through once and then write it from memory. The text is short—25 words—and says in part: *our entire neighborhood*. Each time, for the past 10 years or so, 85 to 95 percent of the participants drop the word *entire*. When analyzing their responses, they often express surprise they dropped that word, but upon reflection they realize that unconsciously they experienced the felt knowing that the word *entire* is redundant in that context.

English novelist, short story writer, essayist, and librettist E.M. Forester understands this *concealment* when he writes, "How do I know what I think until I see what I say?" (71). But neuroscientist David Eagleman in his lucid book *Incognito: The Secret Lives of the Brain* nails it best: "There is a looming chasm between what your brain knows and what your mind is capable of accessing" (55). Eagleman talks about what he calls *implicit memory,* information in the brain that the mind cannot quite get out. He quotes psychologist Hermann Ebbinghaus, "most of these experiences remain concealed from consciousness and yet produce an effect which is significant and which authenticates their previous experience" (57).

We know this—Michael Polanyi labels it *tacit* (91–92)—we know we know something but we just can't quite explain it, can't get to it. So we give it labels: *tacit, concealed knowing, the unconscious, subconscious, secret.* Nevertheless, during the act of writing this is exactly what the critical writer must do—"unconceal" those hidden experiences to truly tap meaning.

But unconcealment is tricky business. Not focal, these fuzzy meanings do not sit in waiting. Rather, as Perl describes it, they emerge the way "other bodily processes come—the way sleep comes, or emotions come, or tears come—as we make room for the body to express itself or by allowing the rhythm of bodily processes to take over" (2). Thus writing behavior comes about because of the writer's own activity.

The Unconcealed Revealed in Kindergarten

Participating in the obligatory kindergarten "growing a seed" experience, Ross dutifully folded his two papers into fourths and placed his name and date at the top. The teacher gave each child a bean, a cup, another cup with water, and some soil. They were to plant the seed, water it, place it near the window, tend it, and record what they observed every day (fig. 1.1).

Exemplar, Ross's expository text called "My Seed" shows in microcosm the concept of unconcealment. The lesson lies buried in the soil, so Ross uses the experience to uncover the meaning. He watches his seed grow and he writes. But as is often the case during inquiry, the results are unexpected. So, too, with Ross's inquiry. His seed literally goes sour. Already by "Day 2—it is drke," a telling observation but one Ross does not yet understand. Ross continues to write (and water and water and water) his seed. There is still hope in Ross's writing when he returns from the weekend as his "seed is groing bigr root." Alas, the truth is unconcealed on "Day

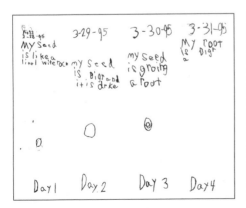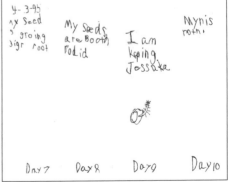

Figure 1.1. My Seed

8—My seeds are both rodid." The meaning concealed in the dark seed from Day 2 comes to Ross through his writing. Assigned to help Jessica, he draws his conclusion on "Day 10, Myn is roth."

Through this lens, the total mind-brain environment (including writing behavior) is at once paradoxically simple and complex. In this way, the process of writing, guided by personal momentum and experienced as inquiry, moves forward by going back. What Emig calls "recursive" is what Perl and Egendorf call "writer-based retrospective structuring" (260) and that cycle becomes a necessary tool for the critical writer.

The Unconcealed Revealed in High School

Inquiry, good inquiry has nothing to do with genre. In fact a case may be made for all writing to include, be the result of, or be inspired by good inquiry. (See Chapter 5.) In *Acts of Teaching,* first edition, we included three selections by Chris Allen, a high school student and eager writer. His initial draft

> It has snowed again.
> The world is crackling with ice.
> I see death at every icicle.
> There is the deer who tried to jump the fence last night.
> Her leg caught and she hung there until she froze to death.
> I see the death and think of my father in South America.
> Children are being killed by stray bullets.
> Stray bullets and freak snow storms.
> They both kill.

Two great ideas roll around here. One part observation: the ice and deer caught on wire; one part experiential: previous knowledge built around his father, a military man in South America. Lacking a focused topic, Chris needed to develop some questions for himself as a writer. So Eddie encouraged him to take notes about the details of what he knew about both ideas. After that, he encouraged Chris to engage in that critical piece of making predictions. In the process Chris realized that while one image reminded him of the actions of another unrelated event, neither really belonged together.

So he investigated snow and ice and freezing weather. He read articles about how animals survive (or not) in harsh extremes. He called his father and interviewed him, asking some difficult questions about surviving in a war-torn environment. His inquiry allowed him to move his prewriting into two different directions. He evaluated his findings and began to organize his thinking into two very different shapes, so two very different poems emerged—both born of and bettered by inquiry. He developed the first into a narrative somewhat lyrical poem.

Another Freezing Season
Snowmen made of soil and unclean snow decompose
As children with red noses
Watch in frustration
From behind smeared windows.
Maple trees crackle free
From their icy bondage
And jagged chinks of crystallized death
Shatter on the wet pavement.
An icicle of blood dissolves from the nose of a frozen deer,
Its body hanging stiffly from a barbed wire fence.
Too high for its legs to conquer.
Decay drifts from the breaths of cracked-filled sidewalks
As the sun lifts
The souls of a million different identities.
My eyes fill with tears
From the rising, moist air,
And blur the magnificent sight of
Another winter's steam bath.
Pine trees no longer emit laughter or screams from
Clumps of swirling wind, but instead
Whisper mild breezes through their
Needle-laden tongues.
My younger brother smuggles snow into our house
At an attempt to salvage the crippling scene.
I watch all this while
A blue truck speeds by
Showering my lawn with gray, aging slush.

Which slaps an image onto my chapped face and I sit
   quietly,
Disquieted at the thought of another dying season.
                                             —Chris Allen

Chris creates a more complete picture of a world covered in
an extreme ice storm. He places his poetic persona in the middle
of the image even while making an oblique allusion to Rudolph the
Red-Nosed Reindeer. He allows for a certain passage of time. After
his inquiry, he realized something he said he knew but "in the back
of my mind," about how ice and snow changes and how that could
be symbolic and how it made him feel—that felt sense—about the
importance of this experience. Remarkably, the placement of the
little brother adds an irony to the whole tableau.

There are constant dichotomies of images and metaphors in
Chris's new writing: the irony of screaming play juxtaposed with the
whispering winds, the brother trying to hold onto something that
cannot be held, the maturity of the persona against the naiveté of
the brother, the tragic and deadly result than can happen amid the
beauty of a winter snow. The quality of Chris's inquiry rises up in the
lexicon throughout the entire manuscript: "crystallized," "steam
bath," "needle-laden," "dying season."

This poem resulted because of reading and observation
and examination. Chris went beyond the cursory. And for his
ending, he read about the seasons, coming across information
about how late winter storms totally kill things unexpectedly.
That knowledge allowed him to make connections and metaphors
and images he could not have done without the inquiry, without
the depth.

But it is his second writing that is perhaps more powerful
and more intense if not more important. In this manuscript he uses
the genre of concrete poetry to ensure the clarity of his meaning.
Connecting the dots does for the reader exactly what the writer has
done. During the interview with his father, who was stationed in
South America, he told Chris some of the things happening to
children and families in a war-torn environment.

Chris takes the notion of the game of playing connect the dots
with gunfire and the actual things he discovered—mainly that children

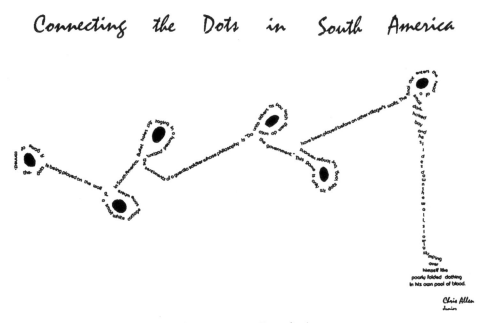

Figure 1.2. Connecting the Dots in South America

are victims of tragedy in war. This is his result, his unconcealment (fig. 1.2).[1]

We think the analogy James Britton used to describe retrospective structuring fitting here: "the sculptor with chisel in hand must both cut and observe the effect of his cut before going on" (in Freedman, 64). Hence, the writer must both write the words and in the act of almost spontaneous shaping consider the effect of those words before moving on. The writer must both feel and think the words. This is what we mean by the "felt sense" of the critical writer.

WHO IS THE CRITICAL WRITER?

Characterized by an ability to carefully discern or judge his or her writing by showing depth of insight about the topic, holding to marked standards, and using appropriate strategies, a critical writer makes the proper emendations during prewriting, while drafting, and most certainly during the revising process, regardless of the genre. In other words, the critical writer uses his or her "felt sense" continually throughout the writing process.

The critical writer also engages in what Britton calls "projective structuring" (Freedman, 64)—the ability to shape the material out of the ephemeralness of a generative idea in such a way that the reader "gets it." Thus, critical writing joins hands with inquiry—that seeking after truth, that process of unconcealment, that asking questions of self to produce logical and carefully honed papers. Together they produce meaning.

HOW DOES THE CRITICAL WRITER EMPLOY HEURISTICS?

The word *heuristics* even sounds Greek. *Heuriskein,* meaning "to discover" or "to find," reaches us over the centuries as a procedure or a guide in solving a problem. Here in this text, we use the term to describe a process that moves thinking and writing from the simple to the complex and perhaps back again to the simple to yet again venture to the complex—like taking the mind by the hand and leading it around corners.

Education has employed heuristics throughout its history. Young children begin with easy concepts but as they cognitively mature, the concepts increase in complexity. Consider the concept of the number *one,* once mastered, little children return to the concept again in the numbers *eleven, twenty-one,* and so on. The heuristics suggested in this book offer progressive problem-solving skills that enable—even invite—exploration to stimulate deeper thinking or paths to penetrate language in ways that yield insightful meaning for experiences, literature, and research.

The Carroll/Wilson Inquiry Schemata model (fig. 1.3) provides a practical and systematic journey throughout inquiry, but it also provides a heuristic for any type of writing. This provides the foundational piece upon which to build any genre.

By internalizing appropriate heuristics, critical writers balance their writing on the fulcrum of critical consciousness coupled with previous knowledge, experiences, and observations. Donald A. Schön would call this "reflection-in-action." The notion of students thinking about what they are writing even while they are in the act of writing (the sculptor with chisel in hand) enhances both

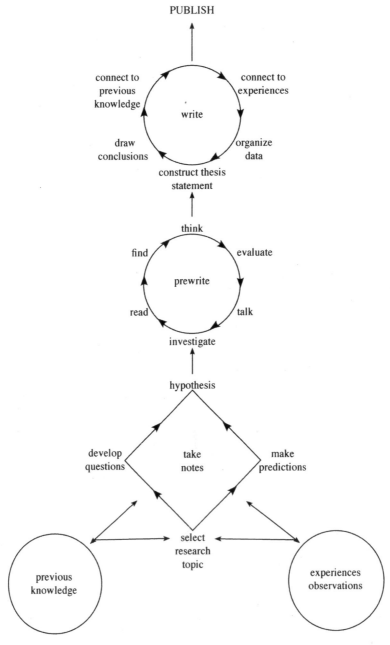

Figure 1.3. The Carroll/Wilson Inquiry Schemata

the thinking and the writing. It creates what Michael Strong calls "intellectual habits" (14). Heuristics give writers a way to focus and refocus and, if need be, focus yet again, or, as Schön says, "they turn thought back on action and on the knowing which is implicit in action" (50). Students may continually ask themselves an entire taxonomy of questions as they write, for example:

> Why am I writing this?
> Who is my audience?
> What is their age, educational level? Where do they live?
> How do I want my audience to feel?
> What do I want my audience to think?
> What do I want my audience to do after reading what I have written?
> What genre—story, poem, play, essay—will best convey my meaning?
> Are these the best, most precise words, to transmit my meaning?
> Is that image I created apt?
> Will a comma, dash, or parenthesis work best in this context?
> What do I mean?
> Does this make sense?

Here's where discernment surfaces. The student tries to make sense of the act of writing, by reflecting *on* the writing *during* the writing. A critical writer literally dialogues with self. To paraphrase Donald Murray's description of this kind of critical thinking: The self speaks, the other self listens and responds. The self proposes; the other self considers. The self makes, the other self evaluates. The two selves collaborate: a problem is spotted, discussed, defined; solutions are proposed, rejected, suggested, attempted, tested, discarded, accepted (142).

Such a dialogue-with-self heuristic might go something like this:

> *I am writing this piece to try to understand why I get so angry when I get bad customer service.*
> *I don't know who my audience is right now other than maybe myself—maybe I just need to vent. No, actually,*

*I'd like store managers to hear what I have to say. So
maybe some kind of business magazine would work or
a letter.*

*This needs to be persuasive because when the readers finish,
I want them to change some business tactics.*

*I think I'll just write out the vent first and see where it takes
me. I want it short but with punch. Business people aren't
going to read a long, drawn out diatribe.*

*I'll have to be careful not to attack but to persuade. I have to
mean what I say. I have to know what I mean.*

Through reflection, deeper understandings emerge, which,
in turn, emboldens further writing, deeper revisions, better word
choices—in short—intelligent, critical writing.

CONCLUDING MUSINGS

Whenever we are working on a book, it amazes us how something
related will present itself and say, "Here I am." Recently, we received
this stunning piece of discourse from Senga Rounds, a trainer from
Northside ISD in San Antonio.

> The contents of the *Acts of Teaching* preface weigh heavily on
> me. I attended school in the Caribbean where the educational
> system relied heavily on the product paradigm. My earliest
> school memories are inundated with the horrors of spelling
> tests, endless drills and bland worksheets. Week after week
> we took our spelling lists home and labored over them. We
> received one lash, down our backs with the strap, for every
> word we spelled incorrectly. Our classes were as orderly as
> our starched uniforms, crisp white socks and polished shoes.
> We sat quietly in rows, listened while the teacher lectured,
> and we wrote three-page essays from standard prompts. We
> analyzed and eloquently quoted Shakespeare.
>
> For a long time, even at the start of my teaching career,
> I was convinced that I went through one of the greatest
> educational systems ever. I would argue with my colleagues
> about their practices bringing up examples such as, "We were
> always well behaved." We always did our homework." "We could
> read Shakespeare at eleven years old."

I saw the truth a mere three years ago. The product paradigm does not work; rather it has the opposite effect. Nothing hurts me more than the idea of what others endured in that school system. The practices worked for me because I was a natural reader. By age seven or so, I didn't need prompting to pick up a book. Books were my life. As a result, my vocabulary and writing skills increased. These product paradigm practices didn't work for those who struggled with reading. Students were beaten day after day, week after week, and year after year of their school life. They were blamed for their learning deficiencies and relegated to remedial classes, where the teacher gave them coloring sheets while she sat at her desk ignoring them. My fellow students were labeled as failures for the remainder of their lives while the "bright" ones were revered and given special treatment.

To those who succeeded and to some on the outside, our school system surpassed most of the school systems in other countries. What about all those students who left school with nothing more than the belt marks on their backs? The product paradigm failed, for them and also for everyone like me who believed that we were a part of something great. Now I get to be a part of what true learning should be. Maybe one day I can return and show the others back home how it really should be done.

While we were deep into writing about the notions of recursiveness, projective structuring, writer-based retrospective structuring, and unconcealment in inquiry, along comes the perfect of example of the theory.

Here's the backstory: Senga, in culminating her required reading of *Acts of Teaching* to become a trainer for Abydos Literacy Learning (ALL), held a mirror up to her own educational experience. Her serious consideration and the writing about it bent back the years and unconcealed the memories. Her personal narrative held the inquiry within it—the going back to come forward—the Caribbean educational system, the status it has held, "our school system surpassed most of the school systems in other countries," the realization, maybe even a surprise for someone who "was convinced that I went through one of the greatest educational systems ever." Finally, the *piece de résistance*, "Maybe one day I can return and show the others back home how it really should be done."

Senga makes our point with power and grace. It seems to us that all writing, in whatever genre, ultimately becomes a process of discovery. To be philosophical, writing becomes a process of what Heidegger calls "unconcealment" or what the Greeks called *alêtheia,* which literally means "not-concealed" or "the truth." Senga, through her writing, proves that to be true.

Clearly Senga was being prepared for a dictatorship, not a democracy.

NOTE

1. Figure reads (left to right): A game of connect-the-dots is being played on the wall of a small white cottage some where in South America. Bullet holes zig-zaging in a hurried pattern, the sentiments of a guerilla soldier whose philosophy is "Do unto others as you wish them do unto the government." This game is only six dots long, but longer versions have been played before on other villager's walls. The final dot enters the head of a small dark-haired boy and he slides down the wall slowly slumping over himself like poorly folded clothing in his own pool of blood.

Chris Allen
Junior

THE CRITICAL WRITER AND INQUIRY

INQUIRY VERSUS RESEARCH

Most agree that the word *inquiry* has replaced the word *research* in the academic language of many schools today. An apt replacement as *inquiry* suggests the act of seeking out information whereas *research* suggests a more formal investigation into references and sources. While both may end up with new conclusions, a report, a presentation, or even a paper, *inquiry* centers on the process, not the product. And it is that process that ultimately hooks students, leading them deeper and deeper into their thinking and knowing. To paraphrase Ellin Oliver Keene, this entire approach to a topic or subject provides students with a prelude to the capacity of their minds, their intellect, their "joy of understanding" (21). In our words, this entire approach, this back and forth movement over a topic, allows for depth and the gradual unconcealment of what all of us in the teaching profession glibly call *making sense.*

We can thank Lev Vygotsky, the Russian cognitive developmentalist, for his ZPD, "zone of proximal development." His notion of a zone or area in between where a student is and where the student should, could, or wants to be gives us the theory behind scaffolding, which is the trendy term for a *heuristic*. His theory frees us to invite a heuristic approach to the process of inquiry and allows students the time it takes to engage in true inquiry.

During the inquiry process, students don't take quantum leaps from topic to paper—copying bits and pieces from hither and yon then sewing them together for the typical somewhat plagiarized "research paper." Rather in true inquiry. Students move—some quickly, some ploddingly—through Vygotsky's heuristic of concept development. They begin with "topical heaping": a *trial and error* period of prewriting—maybe even doodling—usually characterized by a gathering of random findings including things, perhaps forgotten things, tucked inside their brains. They add information from their *line of vision,* that is what they notice and deem important to their topic at that moment (albeit not always connected), and they engage in *rearrangement,* a moving around, where connections are chancy—a kind of incoherent coherence.

Then the novice inquirer enters what Vygotsky calls "complexes." As suggested by the term, complexes take writers into more complicated interconnections. Here writers make connections in several different ways: *associations,* where they group content by similarities; *collections,* where they group data by differences (important when considering other points of view); *chains* (common in inquiry) where a piece of meaning leads to more meaning or deeper meaning or leads to the need for more information on the subject; and finally writers often experience *diffuse complexes* where substantive connections become fluid, uneven, and sometimes startling, but illuminating. Here we find the proverbial "aha"! the Eureka! These complexes have a way of propelling writers forward for they provide the intellectual challenge and excitement that stimulates the brain.

The bridge to concepts is often marked by "pseudo-concepts," those quasi concepts that resemble genuine understanding, but are sometimes necessary along the road to true inquiry. But here is exactly where students need intervention. We are reminded of advice once rendered in lecture by Emig, "It is just as important not to intervene at the wrong time as it is important to intervene at the right time."

During the pseudo-conceptual stage, knowledgeable teachers nudge and prod students. They invite students to explain their findings, flesh out their information, support what they say with textual evidence—testimony, statistics, facts, anecdotes, explanations, descriptions, details—the stuff of a good solid inquiry. Then and only then will novice investigators reach what Vygotsky calls a "genuine concept" that results in a true understanding of the topic under investigation. This is true inquiry.

THE CARROLL/WILSON INQUIRY SCHEMATA MODEL

Based on years of personal research, which resulted in several books, as well as years of reading and studying the research of others, most specifically in the field of education and educational psychology, we formulated our schemata—a model heuristic or scaffold upon which inquiry may be hung. (See fig. 1.3.) By its very nature, our model provides an outline upon which may be superimposed variations and recursivities that rise up during the process. Not static but dynamic, it gives students both the zone and the needed time to conduct true inquiry. Students begin easy enough with what they know and proceed upward and inward to a true depth of inquiry. Radically different than the way we typically teach "research" in schools, this approximates the genuine pulling and tugging, the giving and giving up that happens during the inquiry process.

In Chapter 4, Travis Leech, an ELAR teacher in Northside ISD in San Antonio, Texas, shows us how he actually implemented our schemata with his middle school students. But in this chapter we offer a detailed explanation of our schemata.

TAPPING THE RIGHT "STUFF"

Each piece of the schemata stands as a mini-schema. For example, the bottom two circles represent myriad possibilities, directions the inquiry might take; they embody Vygotsky's unorganized heaps. This is the generative phase of inquiry. The circle on the left calls upon previous knowledge. No student comes to inquiry *tabula rasa,* a blank slate as the Latin term suggests, but rather students come with all manner of random tidbits tucked into the folds of their brains, tidbits just as convoluted and complex as those folds. Not to validate this knowing is to ignore not only potential ideas galore but also sparks ready to ignite into specific topics of interest.

The circle on the right empowers the student even more. Tapping experiences and observations often illuminates that niggling notion, that smoldering thought, that uneasiness. How sad to go into classrooms where teachers pass out topics to students with little regard for the students' previous knowledge, experiences, or observations, never mind interest or need. It's a bit like giving out restroom passes willy-nilly—the implication: Go now whether you need to or not. Why would anyone, let alone a distracted insecure adolescent, want to spend hours researching an assigned topic as irrelevantly esoteric as "The water imagery in John Donne's poetry"? That topic may turn on an English teacher, but it holds little allure for a 21st century 16-year-old. So they have no alternative but to cut and paste the words of others. If we want true inquiry, the answer lies in those two bottom circles and lots of prewriting.

In our book *Acts of Teaching,* we elaborate on many prewriting techniques—from easy warm-ups to prewriting for finding a topic; from rhetorical strategies to techniques for analyzing literature. Through one, some, or all of these strategies, students begin to uncover what they know and need to know so they can hone topics. As we always say, adapting that wonderful opening line from the poem referenced in Chapter 1, "Valentine for Ernest Mann": You can't order a topic the way you order a taco! Students—all involved in inquiry—do a better job if they write their way into the specificity of topic.

TAKING STOCK OF THINGS

All arrows emanating out of the previous knowledge, experiences, and observations circles point to "select research topic" and to the diamond (symbolism intended) that moves students from the random acts of possible unconcealment into those complexes where Vygotsky suggests the writer finds similarities, differences, and connections. This gathering phase of inquiry is marked by tentativeness here— the questions, the predictions, the notes—all of which leads to a hypothesis, which we call the "working thesis statement" (WTS). It, too, rises up as tentative at this point. Those arrows invite a stopping and taking stock of what they have "heaped" in their prewriting. Taking stock really is the first and important step for the critical writer. The prewriting is just that—a prelude. Taking stock means reading over everything carefully with that developing critical eye. It means appraising, assessing what has been written to estimate what is valuable. Only after a proper appraisal can students make a commitment, however provisional, to a specific topic.

With that topic in mind, students commence taking notes, developing questions, making predictions. This is nothing more intimidating than the famous K-W-L Chart of elementary school taken to its true sophistication. The task is clear: Figure out what you know, what you want to know, and what you have learned. Use that learning to craft a WTS—a working thesis statement, emphasis at this point on *working*. In the elementary and middle school, we call the thesis statement the central or controlling idea. As our housekeeper says, "same same."

Although they already have much writing under their belts, students are not there yet. At this point they flounder around in pseudo-concepts and often don't know it. The high point of this stage is their hypothesis, but their hypothesis is just that—a work in progress on its way to becoming a working thesis statement.

NOW THE WORK BEGINS

A hypothesis, literally something lurking under the thesis, has evolved to mean a guide in investigating. It's a proposition working its way into becoming the thesis. (See the word *thesis* snuggled into the word *hypothesis*?) So it's time to talk about the investigation, time to hear other points of view, time to test. Moving into the prewriting and drafting phase, further prewriting based on reading and thinking and more talking and sharing leads to finding more specifics, more details, more arguments, and finally to evaluating. All of this takes work; however if done correctly, this hard intellectual work carries with it deep engagement and fervor.

Sometimes at this point in the process, the entire idea is trashed. Some students begin anew, revisiting the schemata in their search. Most of the time, though, the idea is honed, or extended, rearranged, or refashioned in some way. But that which is concealed often remains hidden, needing more critical thought, more digging, more reading, more writing before its unconcealment.

Many regard the last circle "write" in the schemata the difficult circle, but they are probably not writers, for writers know that the "prewrite" circle proves the most taxing. "Writing is pre-writing," the axiom goes. Donald Murray claims prewriting "usually takes about 85% of the writer's time. It includes the awareness of his world from which the subject is born" ("Teach Writing as a Process Not Product," 4). That awareness undergoes scrutiny now; figuratively speaking, it is placed under the microscope of the writer's mind. In inquiry, this part of the process calls upon the writer to be critical. Here the rubber meets the road; here what has been written becomes the challenge as the writer undergoes the mental processes referenced in Chapter 1. Here the writer has to make sense of this new idea—this WTS—so that an audience will also make sense of it. Quite literally, the ephemerality of talk and thought must transmogrify into substance, words with meaning, words with that felt sense. Here the writer both grapples with and dwells in the idea. Like Aladdin with his lamp, all that rubbing finally produces the genie—the genuine concept, the thesis statement.

WRITING AS A MODE OF LEARNING

At this point in the inquiry process, the finishing phase, students use their newly constructed and well-honed, well-crafted theses statements that grew out of their WTS to focus their papers or presentations. (See Carroll, "Teaching the Thesis.") Clearly now, all the heaping, prewriting, evidence, facts, statistics, personal anecdotes, details, descriptions, definitions, examples, explanations, and textual evidence can be organized with conclusions and supporting data in the proper places. Only after all that is in place can the students coherently connect it to previous knowledge in some way, connect it to experiences in some way, organize their data and writing in some way, and draw conclusions.

Finally ready for publication, the publishing phase, the work is presented to the teacher, the class, displayed in some way, or better yet sent out to the public.

CONCLUDING MUSINGS

Musing One

After working with inquiry and students on various levels, it has become clear to us that there is a missing piece. Believers in students "doing" not just "getting," we adamantly recommend that following the students working through the Carroll/Wilson Inquiry Schemata Model, they reflect upon that process and create their own schemata. This places the crown upon the head of critical thinking. This is what Keene calls "seeking understanding in our minds" (20). Encouraging uniqueness, each schema will be unique, but each schema will tell students how their minds work (or didn't), allowing them the freedom of knowing about their knowing—what we call in the field *metacognition.*

Students who know their processes, who embrace them, are not shaken or discouraged by them. Rather, they have their own "text structures" that give them confidence and security.

Musing Two

All this emphasis upon inquiry may lead those teachers who treat research as an event to think that the strategies offered here should be covered when "doing the research paper." We want to make something clear: inquiry belongs in all writing.

Good writers of all genres employ inquiry and so should students. We see inquiry in good essays such as the recent one in the *New York Times Magazine* by Wil S. Hylton entitled "Lights, Action: The Alternative Realities of James Turrell." But we expect inquiry in such an essay. Yet Nancy Willard's poem "How to Stuff a Pepper" has inquiry stuffed into those "green buttocks" (Carroll & Wilson, P.A.L., 56), and Kathi Appelt's "Ode to My Southern Drawl" (Carroll & Wilson, P.A.L., 66) rings with inquiry about the *literati,* "coldsnap" or her reference to the Biblical Luke.

Musing Three

Warning: This is not a five-day process as some who don't engage in inquiry or who don't write or who try to oversimplify a deeply complicated process or who worry more about covering the curriculum than teaching students conceptually often try to do. If collapsed into five days, the inquiry will be superficial or plagiarized. There will be no engagement, no unconcealment, no felt sense, no habit of thought, no investment, no reflection, no real inquiry. In short, it will be only five wasted days with students learning wrong things about true inquiry.

Musing Four

"Do not confine your children to your own learning for they were born in another time," so goes an old Hebrew proverb, reminding us to remind our readers not to confine inquiry to one genre for it was born in another time. Inquiry as an ongoing process belongs side-by-side with writing as a process. It's like the old song lyric, "you can't have one without the other." Or perhaps more literary, William Butler Yeats asks us to consider, "How do we know the dancer from the dance"?

> A writer is a person whose best is released in the accomplishment of writing. . . . He does not necessarily think these things—he does not, that is, think them out and then write them down: he writes, and the best of him, in spite even of his thought, will appear on the page even to his surprise, unrecognized or even sometimes against his will, by proper use of words.
>
> —William Carlos Williams

 # THE PEDAGOGY OF THE CRITICAL WRITER

A GLANCE BACK IN TIME

We find it interesting to note from the lofty perspective of time how logically we have moved from years of work on writing as a process in the latter part of the 20th century to this 21st century dwelling on inquiry and deeper understandings. And it seems our colleagues in the field of brain research have moved in that direction as well. No longer satisfied with the observable workings of the brain or the structures of the conscious mind, neuroscientists now navigate the deeper levels of the subconscious. As David Eagleman writes, "The brain works its machinations in secret, conjuring ideas like tremendous magic. It does not allow its colossal operating system to be probed by conscious cognition. The brain runs its show incognito" (7).

Now we want to know all about that incognito brain and how it affects our writing.

In the 1970s and 1980s, we were all about getting students comfortable with the act of writing, with getting words down that approximated their experiences and observations. We wanted them to have solid text structures upon which to build stories, essays, and poems. We wanted clarity and aptness—we wanted voice. What we got was what Janet Emig calls "surface scrapings" (46).

Today we build on those earlier experiences and studies. They form the platform for a new way of looking at writing—writing richer and more dimensional. Just as we are no longer satisfied with black and white two-dimensional films, we pay extra for those three-dimensional ones—or better yet the stereoscopic 3D or Blu-ray 3D, the "next gen." We want to be there in that virtual world. So, too, with writing. No longer satisfied with the perfunctory paper-a-week, we want critical writers who explore their writing and thinking in an effort to tease out *the making sense,* the 3-D, that deeper dimension with its surprises and depth of understanding.

Enter Ken Macrorie.

In a book published in 1980, long before its time, he introduced the I-Search Paper.

> Contrary to most school research papers, the I-Search comes out of a student's life and answers a need in it. The writer testifies to the subjective-objective character of the project. The paper is alive, not borrowedly inert. Writing it, many students for the first time find that writing is a way of thinking, of objectifying an act that has counted for them. As the sentences go down on the page, they become both finished statements and starting points for reflection and evaluation. The passages grow with thought. (ii)

The brilliance of the clause "they become both finished statements" juxtaposed with the phrase "starting points" suggests the interlacing structure of critical writing. Agglutinated in one sentence, the oxymoronic notion of "finished" yet "starting" captures the simultaneity of thinking and writing, writing and thinking, and the recursiveness of both. Macrorie calls this process "searching writing."

The "Search" in Searching Writing

The search of the critical writer begins on the page. It begins freely, writing quickly—a wind sucking memories from the brain as the hand moves. We began with listing. As we say in *Acts of Teaching,* "Listing calls upon both the left and right side of the brain because lists may be logical with one thing following the other in sequential order, or they may be serendipitous with one item causing an unexpected turn, a surprising thought, or an intriguing possibility" (16). Listing is Vygotsky's diffuse complexes in action.

As an example, we invited students to write the ABCs vertically down a page. When finished we encouraged them to write any connections with each letter as it popped into their heads. If nothing happened, they simply moved on. But they could go back and make associations with the letter later or not at all.

Because teachers should always model, I did this exercise, too. My first associations looked like this:

A　aging, Aunt Helen
B　Beach Haven, birthday parties, books
C　coffee
D　dogs

I shared my list followed by students doing the same. We talked about the experience and decided to let the list rest for a bit. "Often with listing, the idea does not lie in something actually listed by rather in the exploration of the connections among the words, phrases, or sentences on the lists. The idea may hide between the lines . . . as if the idea resides in the spaces . . . not in the words themselves" (*Acts,* 17).

Another day we went back for another go. This time I added:

A　Mom
B　ball blocks
C　coloring books I hated—wanted to make my own pictures
D　Dairy Cream, Charlie Dusko

Charlie Dusko jumped off the page like some animated character, frantically waving at me. Why I hadn't thought of Charlie in over a half century! What was he doing on my list—this weird neighborhood kid, raised by his grandmother? He came to school and sat on the windowsill contentedly chewing the long rope-like pulls that controlled the shades. What fold in my brain held that image? What truth did I want to uncover? That he was the first mentally challenged kid I knew? That I thought it cruel when the kids called him "monkey"? Where were his parents? I told the kids that I needed to write more to unconceal what was concealed in this memory.

So we did some freewriting. Students love to freewrite. Amazingly when they freewrite, they write authentically and they write surprises. (Note, though, this freewriting was not out of the blue—grab a pencil and paper and begin freewriting—but rather became the next step in a heuristic built upon the simple ABCs and random associations.)

What might come of this first foray into freewriting: a poem, a memoir, a brief piece of personal narrative, an essay on how kids with disabilities used to be treated, or nothing? Only more writing and inquiry will tell the tale.

Inquiry as the Search

Quite naturally out of this deceptively simple task of "doing the ABCs" (those bottom two circles on the schemata model), I used that momentum to teach the characteristics of the different genres. This heightened the excitement of the inquiry process because students realized they had choices—and—as we always say, choice equals voice.

So again I shared with the students my topic choice for the freewrite—Charlie Dusko. Candidly, I admitted that I was unsure of the genre at this point, and I was definitely not sure of my focus, my thesis. I told the students, "It is time for me to ask myself questions. I think I know what I know but there is much I want to know all of a sudden about this kid Charlie and how he connects to me. There is much I want to learn."

So I began reading about how mentally disabled people were treated in the 1930s and 1940s. I learned they were removed from society and put in places with names like "insane asylums," and were called names like "feebleminded" or "lunatic." Did I know this when I was 8 or 10? Did I hear my parents talking about these things? I wrote, Maybe Mom and Aunt Helen discussed Charlie, but I know they didn't talk about sterilization—still I remember them talking quite animatedly about the Kennedy sister who was given a lobotomy, but that was later and I was older. Did that get connected in my mind to Charlie? My inquiry led me to 1941 and the Kennedy girl's name, Rosemary. Rosemary Kennedy, the president's sister, was given a lobotomy in 1941 but nobody talked about it—few even knew about it then. Still I probed: How does Rosemary connect to Charlie in my mind? So much critical thinking, honest and authentic, happened next.

Answers to some questions led me to other questions. I took copious notes that filled my binder. And without thinking much at the moment about any schemata, I realized the need to talk.

And so the inquiry process continued. Eventually, I wrote a paper entitled simply "Charlie." An expository essay of sorts, it wound around a personal narrative. Here is a slice of it:

Charlie

Of all my classmates Charlie stands out, and I am not sure why. The year was 1945. World War II ended in May and soon after Charlie moved in with his grandmother next door to our rambling Victorianesque home on Washington Road. I remember how strange he looked and I remember my mother advising me "Don't pay much attention to Charlie, Junch. He's different."

In 1945 people didn't know much about mental illness and kids knew even less. We weren't even that far away from 19th Century witch-hunts, madhouses, and places like Bedlam where people paid a penny to watch so-called inmates as entertainment. Those suffering were thought to either be possessed by the devil or crazy—a middle English term meaning "cracked."

The turn of the century brought new terrors: insane asylums, lobotomies, shock treatments, and doses and shots of experimental drugs—all things we didn't know let alone talk about. So Charlie being "different" meant nothing to me as a kid of 8. So why do I remember him so vividly?

"Different" described Charlie to a tee. He looked odd with his wide face and big head—not too big but a you-notice-it big. His arms dangled, reminding me of a puppet while his long legs and small feet made him slightly grotesque. I obeyed Mom and basically didn't pay him any mind.

When school opened in September, Charlie was placed in my third-grade classroom. Mrs. Francy, the quintessential forbearing teacher, sat him directly in front of her desk. But Charlie would have none of it and soon jumped to the wooden windowsill where he perched all day staring out the window and chewing on the cord that open and closed the shades. It was hard to obey Mom then and ignore him.

"Monkey! Monkey!" the kids would taunt him when Mrs. Francy was out of earshot. I hated hearing that. "Monkey! Monkey!" they would whisper to him on line. I hated hearing that. It made my stomach turn upside down—it was like watching someone hit a puppy or pull wings off a fly. Defenseless, Charlie suffered. Defenseless, I suffered, too.

When I read this to the students, one asked, "Were you afraid of Charlie?" Talk about a bombshell. Talk about the power of writing groups. At that moment, at that very second, I got it. The meaning unconcealed itself, and I wanted to explain it.

"No," I answered, "I wasn't afraid of Charlie, I realize now because of this writing and your question that I was just afraid. Being an eight-year-old at that time equaled a naiveté about such things. But when I began the writing, I realized how my mom and aunt recoiled from the idea of a lobotomy. I remember asking, 'What's a lobotomy?'

'They drill a hole in the front of your head,' Aunt Helen tossed my way.

I remembered Mom saying, 'They have so much money, why would they do that to her?' I remember being frightened—not that my family would do that to me but that any family would do that to any child. I remember wondering if that's what happened to Charlie."

That's when my entire inquiry process revealed the truth. All this writing and thinking and talking and sharing came down to this: a sudden realization that people are fragile and often at the mercy of other people. The innocence and invincibility of youth was gone forever.

Searching Writing and the C-W Schemata

Taking Macrorie's "searching writing" and superimposing it upon our schemata model shows them to be similar processes. Writing out of previous knowledge, experiences, and observations and then writing until that prior knowledge connects with and unconceals the truth helps us make sense of things.

Our brains function in two different ways: "One is fast, automatic, and below the surface of conscious awareness, while the other is slow, cognitive, and conscious" (Eagleman, 109). We believe writing is the conduit between these systems. The preceding exercise shows the power of using the first system, which is "automatic, implicit, heuristic, intuitive, holistic, reactive, and impulsive" (Eagleman 109) to communicate with the second system, which is "cognitive, systematic, explicit, analytic, rule-based, and reflective" (Eagleman 109). That deepening produces the profundity, the making sense, the felt sense, the meaning making that characterizes good solid writing.

From I-Search to iSearch

Macrorie's I-Search always was an excellent way to engage student writers in inquiry. We, however, see the need to update and regenerate it into iSearch, which embraces the technology of tablets, smartphones, databases, blogs, and the Internet. From our perspective, iSearch is a natural 21st century evolution from the 20th century personal exploration Macrorie detailed.

The distance 50 years ago between the writer and accessing data proved a monumental chasm. During my undergraduate years I remember conducting research by using the several books that were placed on what was then called "library reserve," books that could be used only in the library. If a student was using them, everyone one else had to wait their turn—in the library. In today's world of instant communications, instant access, instant food, instant replay—indeed instant everything—that system of retrieval must seem quaint, but it accounts in part for the antediluvian use of note cards and elaborate footnotes and references.

Sometimes trying to accomplish the act of inquiry was just plain difficult if not impossible. I remember fellow students trying to explain away late papers to their professors, "But I couldn't get the books. Somebody else hogged them." But with the advent of technology and the Internet that distance has collapsed dramatically.

Thanks to technology and the formulation of mobile devices, we suggest redefining the "I" in Macrorie's I-Search. His notion of the "I"—the self engaged in what the writer wants or needs to know morphs into discoveries that makes sense in the world of the lower case "i." That use of the lower case "i" suggests a redefining of "I" as not just self but also the merging of self and information and Internet.

The first device that held the moniker of the lower case "i" distinguished it as "Internet ready." Our use of the "i" in iSearch suggests that the search is not only Internet ready but also information appropriate and connected in some way to self. Our concept with iSearch starts with the "i" wanting to know, and nano-fast that "i" transacts with the "I" of technology for easy access to information coming quickly in many different forms.

We suggest that iSearch utilize all things digital—blogs, social networks, databases, digital photostories, online questionnaires, and surveys. And the added bonus of using these inquiry avenues is their multigenre approach. iSearching provides a journey into both real and virtual worlds and into many different sources and genres.

Social Networks and Blogs

The following are worth considering when iSearching:

> *43 Things* is a social networking website established as an online goal setting community. It is built on the principles of tagging, rather than creating explicit interpersonal links (as seen in Friendster and Orkut). Users create accounts and then list a number of goals or hopes; these goals are parsed by a lexer and connected to other people's goals that are constructed with similar words or ideas. This concept is also known as folksonomy. Users can set up to 43 goals, and are encouraged to explore the lists of other users and "cheer" them on toward achieving their goals.
>
> *Academia.edu* is a social networking website for academics. It was launched in September 2008 and the site now has over 3 million registered users. The platform can be used to share papers, monitor their impact, and follow the research in a particular field.

Anobii is a social networking site aimed at readers. The service allows individuals to catalogue their books and rate, review, and discuss them with other readers.

Bebo users receive a personal profile page where they can post blogs, photographs, music, videos, and questionnaires that other users may answer. Additionally, users may add others as friends and send them messages, and update their personal profiles to notify friends about themselves.

Blogster is a blogging community that features specific-interest blogs. Blogster maintains an online community of users who publish content, images, video, and more. Blogster members can network and collaborate by creating a blog, building a personalized profile, creating friend lists, commenting on articles, and interacting in an online community. Blogster is positioned on simplicity, and easy-to-use settings options.

Buzznet is a photo, journal, and video-sharing social media network, owned by Buzz Media. Like other social networking sites, Buzznet is a platform for members to share content based on their personal interests. Unlike classic social networking sites, which focus primarily on messaging and profile pages, Buzznet members participate in communities that are created around ideas, events, and interests, most predominantly music, celebrities, and the media.

Care2's stated mission is to help people make the world a better place by connecting them with the individuals, organizations, and responsible businesses making an impact.

DailyBooth was a photoblogging website designed for users to take a photo of themselves every day with a caption, in order to document and share their life with others, thus the slogan "your life in pictures."

Epernicus is a social networking website and professional networking platform resource built by scientists for research scientists. Its main goal is to help scientists to "find the right people with the right expertise at the right time."

Experience Project is a free social networking website of on-line communities premised on connecting people through shared life experiences. With an interactive, user-submitted network of personal stories, confessions, blogs, groups, photos, and videos, the company has collected almost 34 million real-life experiences as of January 2014. Users can join communities organized around experiences and interests, and view shared experiences organized by city and region to connect and interact with people.

Fotki is a digital photo sharing, video sharing, and media social network website and web service suite; it is one of the world's largest social networking sites.

Fotolog.com (changed from Fotolog.net) is a Web 2.0-based shared photoblog web site. With over 30 million registered users, it is one of the oldest and largest sites for sharing pictures through online photo diaries or photo blogs.

The *Goodreads* website allows individuals to freely search Goodreads's extensive user-populated database of books, annotations, and reviews. Users can sign up and register books to generate library catalogs and reading lists.

LibraryThing is a social cataloging web application for storing and sharing book catalogs and various types of book metadata. It is used by individuals, authors, libraries, and publishers.

LifeKnot is a social networking website with a focus on shared interests and hobbies.

Listography is a book and personal web application that allows users to create and share lists. Through list-making, users can shape an autobiography and create references for themselves and others. Some common types of lists are: autobiographical, favorites, motivational, wish lists, to do lists, catalogues, and photo lists. Users are sometimes called listographers and their collection of lists is referred to as the listography.

Open Diary has hosted more than 5 million diaries since it was founded, and continues to be home to over half a million diaries. Currently, there are over 561,000 diaries on Open-Diary.com, including diaries from 77 different countries and all 7 continents. The site innovated some key features that later became central to the architecture of other social networking and blogging sites, including reader comments.

Plurk is a free social networking and microblogging service that allows users to send updates (otherwise known as plurks) through short messages or links, which can be up to 210 text characters in length.

ScienceStage is a global, science-oriented multimedia portal that specializes in online video streaming, which is used to support communication between scientists, scholars, researchers in industry, and professionals. It is also used by academics and students as a virtual educational tool. Video content ranges from conference recordings, to interviews, documentaries, webinars, and tutorials. ScienceStage, as its slogan suggests, also functions as a "hub" by creating a meta-layer that enables the networking of both users (individuals and groups) and content (video, audio, and documents), which forms an integrated multimedia and social networking platform for scientists.

Shelfari is a social cataloging website for books. Shelfari users build virtual bookshelves of the titles they own or have read, and can rate, review, tag, and discuss their books. Users can also create groups that other members may join, create discussions, and talk about books, or other topics. Recommendations can be sent to friends on the site for what books to read.

TeachStreet, Inc. is a website providing information to students on local and online classes and teachers including pricing information, location, and teacher background and training. It also provides online business management tools for teachers and schools.

WeeWorld is an avatar-based massive multi-player online social network. Avatars are called WeeMees. The first WeeMee was created in 2000 and is called Mikey. Anybody can play

WeeWorld although WeeMees under the age of 13 are put on a more strictly monitored version of Weeworld called Weeworld Jr. and must use parental or guardian consent. Users sign up for free and are given a customizable WeeMee, which is a 2-D animated avatar. Users can choose what their WeeMee looks like and its interests. Within the virtual world, users can communicate with other WeeMees by messaging them on home pages or chatting in virtual 2-D worlds, explore the community, as well as play games and participate in quests. Approximately 55 million WeeMees have been created worldwide.

weRead, formerly iRead, is an online community of book enthusiasts.

Wooxie is a social networking website. The website allows users the chance to provide their standard updates with 155 character updates, slightly longer than most other microblogging websites. This is a form of microblogging that enables users to connect people with similar interests.

Social networking sites and blogs act as sounding boards and potential sources of new directions for iSearching because the iSearch allows inquiry to connect on a personal level with others who share the same iSearch. Blogging becomes a writer's notebook for the iSearch. Notes, links, processes are recorded in the blog. Other blogs can be accessed to see many notes, links, and processes. Inquiry does not have to be a solitary act. The iSearch allows for the inquiry to touch others, mean more, and take on dimensions that up until this century the inquirer didn't have ready access to.

Databases

Databases are now easily assessed with iSearching. Some excellent ones are the following:

ABC CLIO deals with issues, understanding controversy, and society. This database helps students develop an in-depth understanding of how society shapes and is shaped by controversy—with authoritative historical context, expert perspectives, and carefully selected primary and secondary sources on the most enduring and timely issues of the day.

Academic Commons is Columbia University's digital repository where faculty, students, and staff of Columbia and its affiliate institutions can deposit the results of their scholarly work and research. Content in Academic Commons is freely available to the public.

Arnetminer is designed to search and perform data mining operations against academic publications on the Internet, using social network analysis to identify connections between researchers, conferences, and publications. This allows it to provide services such as expert finding, geographic search, reviewer recommendation, association search, course search, academic performance evaluation, and topic modeling.

BioOne is an online, full-text database of 171 peer-reviewed scientific journals and books in the biological, ecological, and environmental sciences. Included publications are published by 129 scientific societies, museums, and independent presses.

BASE (Bielefeld Academic Search Engine) is a multidisciplinary search engine to scholarly internet resources, created by Bielefeld University.

The *Directory of Open Access Journals* (DOAJ) is website that lists open access journals and is maintained by Infrastructure Services for Open Access (IS4OA).

Education Resources Information Center (ERIC) is an online digital library of education research and information. ERIC is sponsored by the Institute of Education Sciences of the U.S. Department of Education. The mission of ERIC is to provide a comprehensive, easy-to-use, searchable, Internet-based bibliographic and full-text database of education research and information for educators, researchers, and the general public. Education research and information are essential to improving teaching, learning, and educational decision-making.

GENESIS is a project maintained by the Women's Library at London Metropolitan University. It provides an online database and a list of sources with an intent to support research into women's history.

Index Copernicus (IC) is an online database of user-contributed information, including scientist profiles, as well as of scientific institutions, publications, and projects established in 1999 in Poland. The database has several productivity assessment tools that allow tracking the impact of scientific works and publications, individual scientists, or research institutions. In addition to the productivity aspects, the Index Copernicus also offers the traditional abstracting and indexing of scientific publications.

The *Information Bridge: Department of Energy Scientific and Technical Information* database provides free public access to over 298,000 full-text electronic documents of Department of Energy (DOE) research report literature.

Intute is a free Web service aimed at students, teachers, and researchers in UK further education and higher education. Intute provides access to online resources, via a large database of resources. Each resource is reviewed by an academic specialist in the subject, who writes a short review of between 100 and 200 words, and describes via various metadata fields (such as which subject discipline(s) it will be useful to) what type of resource it is, who created it, who its intended audience is, what time period or geographical area the resource covers, and so on. In July 2010 Intute provided 123,519 records.

Mendeley is a desktop and web program for managing and sharing research papers, discovering research data, and collaborating online. It combines Mendeley Desktop, a PDF and reference management application (available for Windows, Mac, and Linux) with Mendeley Web, an online social network for researchers.

Microsoft Academic Search is a free academic search engine developed by Microsoft Research. It covers more than 48 million publications and over 20 million authors across a variety of domains with updates added each week. This large collection of data has also allowed users to create several innovative ways to visualize and explore academic papers, authors, conferences, and journals.

OAIster was a project of the Digital Library Production Service of the University of Michigan University Library. Its goal is to create a collection of freely available, previously difficult-to-access, academically oriented digital resources that are easily searchable by anyone. OAIster harvests from Open Archives Initiative (OAI)-compliant digital libraries, institutional repositories, and online journals using the Open Archives Initiative Protocol for Metadata Harvesting (OAI-PMH) protocol.

ProQuest provides seamless access to vast content pools which are available to researchers through libraries of all types.

Science.gov is a web portal and specialized search engine. Using federated search technology, Science.gov serves as a gateway to U.S. government scientific and technical information and research. Currently in its fifth generation, Science.gov provides a search of over 38 databases from 14 federal science agencies and 200 million pages of science information with just one query, and is a gateway to 1,900+ scientific websites.

WorldWideScience.org is a global science search engine (academic databases and search engines) designed to accelerate scientific discovery and progress by accelerating the sharing of scientific knowledge. Through a multilateral partnership, WorldWideScience.org enables anyone with Internet access to launch a single-query search of national scientific databases and portals in more than 70 countries, covering all of the world's inhabited continents and over three-quarters of the world's population. From a user's perspective, WorldWideScience.org makes the databases act as if they were a unified whole.

Online Libraries

More exciting is the access to online libraries. These following are just a few:

ARBAonline is the most comprehensive, authoritative database for quality reviews of print and electronic reference works.

The *California Digital Library* (CDL) is the University of California's 11th university library. The CDL was founded to assist the 10 University of California libraries in sharing their resources and holdings more effectively, in part through negotiating and acquiring consortial licenses on behalf of the entire University of California libraries system. Its current mission is to support the assembly and creative use of the world's scholarship and knowledge for the University of California libraries and the communities they serve.

Carrie is an online digital library project based at the University of Kansas containing full-text books and documents.

The Cornell Library Digital Collections (Windows on the Past) are online collections of historical documents. Featured collections include the Database of African-American Poetry, the Historic Math Book Collection, the Samuel May Anti-Slavery Collection, the Witchcraft Collection, and the Donovan Nuremberg Trials Collection.

The *Digital Media Repository* (DMR), established in 2004, is an innovation of Ball State University Libraries. The DMR is a publicly accessible collection of more than 130,000 digital artifacts in 64 browsable and searchable collections. The collection continues to grow at approximately the rate of one new collection per month.

The *Digital Public Library of America* (DPLA) is a project aimed at bringing about a large-scale public digital library. It was launched by Harvard University's Berkman Center for Internet & Society in 2010, with financial support from the Alfred P. Sloan Foundation and several other funders. It "aims to unify such disparate sources as the Library of Congress, the Internet Archive, various academic collections, and presumably any other collection that would be meaningful to include.

ibiblio (formerly SunSITE.unc.edu and MetaLab.unc.edu) is a "collection of collections," and hosts a diverse range of publicly available information and open source content, including software, music, literature, art, history, science, politics, and cultural studies. As an "Internet librarianship," ibiblio is a digital library and archive project. It is run by the School of Information and Library Science and the School of Journalism and Mass Communication at the University of North Carolina at Chapel Hill, with partners including the Center for the Public Domain, IBM, and SourceForge.

Library of Congress Digital Library project

The Library of Congress National Library Program (NDLP) is assembling a digital library of reproductions of primary source materials to support the study of the history and culture of the United States.

Online Gallery—The British Library makes a number of images of items within its collections available online. Its *Online Gallery* gives access to 30,000 images from various medieval books, together with a handful of exhibition-style items in a proprietary format, such as the Lindisfarne Gospels. This includes the facility to "turn the virtual pages" of a few documents, such as Leonardo da Vinci's notebooks. Catalogue entries for a large number of the illuminated manuscript collections are available online, with selected images of pages or miniatures from a growing number of them, and there is a database of significant book bindings.

Open University Library (OU) is researching the use of virtual worlds in teaching and learning and has two main islands in Second Life. In the mid-2010, OU led the list of contributing universities in the number of downloads of its material from the educational resources site iTunes U, with downloads of over 20 million.

Pop Culture Universe: Icons Idols Ideas (PCU) is an irresistible yet authoritative digital database on popular culture in America, both past and present—in a package as dynamic as the topic it covers.

Online Surveys

Another source of inquiry is the online survey. iSearch that utilizes a survey is not only creative but dynamic. Good sources to tap are

2ask
classapps
confirmit
createsurvey
fireflysurvey
inquisite
insightify
intergram
opinionmeter
quicktapsurvey
researchnow
smartsurvey
surveybuilder
surveymonkey
surveysonthego
surveytool
zoomerang

Children-Appropriate Apps

Some apps that are great for children are the following:

Educreation—an app that allows photos, drawings, text, and voice recordings.

Felt Board—students paste their findings here.

Sock Puppets—children can create characters and the voice. Write the dialog and the character speaks it.

Google Glass

But probably the most exciting thing that will allow iSearching to be seamless and have the potential to make inquiry spontaneous and instantaneous is the development of Google Glass. The core of Google Glass is its tiny prism display that sits not in your eye line but above it. The wearer sees the display simply by glancing up. The glasses have camera, microphone, GPS, and use bone induction to give the wearer sound. Wearable computing. Not to mention the iWatch, a 21st century version of the 1940s Dick Tracy 2-Way Wrist Radio, which is on the way. Imagine the potential for iSearches. The wearer needs to know something and with voice command has the ability to access information not only at the fingertips but also with the voice and sight.

iSearching is the act of using technology and the Internet while at the same time carefully filtering and verifying content. iSearch allows for "hard" research—the scientific, fact, statistic, and measurable evidence. Each source must be checked and scrutinized; or for "soft" research—more subjective, opinion-based; plus the hybrid of soft and hard research. Using the facts and figures to support and make opinions, draw conclusions, present a case for something is what inquiry really is all about.

Broader Research Sites

The iSearch should begin with a broad initial research at these possible sites:

> Clusty/Yippy
> DuckDuckGo
> Internet Public Library
> Maholo
> Wikipedia

The Visible Web

The second step is to narrow and deepen the Visible Web iSearch. Probably starts with:

> Ask.com
> Bing
> Google
> USA.gov
> Wolfram Alpha

The Invisible Web

Then the iSearch needs to go to the Invisible Web for deep web searching. Invisible web pages are not spidered by Google. The search continues here:

> Advanced Clusty Searching (meta searching)
> Internet Archive (backward-search past current events)
> Scirus (for scientific searching)

Surfwax (more knowledge focuses and less commerce driven)
U.S. Government Library of Congress

The iSearch then bookmarks and stockpiles all possible content. The piles will then be organized and sifted. Then the iSearch must be filtered and validated. This is the slowest part of the iSearch. But the inquiry must consider these things:

- Author/source and date
- Avoid personal web pages and commercial pages with advertising
- Scientific pages that have scientific advertising
- Dismiss hyperbole and if it sounds too good to be true it is probably fraudulent
- Check the "backlinks" (This is checking the list of incoming hyperlinks from the major websites that recommend the web page of interest. This should give an indication of the reputation of the author.) This is simple to do: go to Google and enter: "link:www.(page's address)" to see the backlinks.

The next stage of the iSearch is to stake a claim. Decide on what has been learned—hence the critical writer. Then find the quotes and cite the content to support the iSearch.

If framed by a hook of a lead and a clincher of an ending the supporting evidence for the clear thesis needs only to be organized and written in an apt progression of ideas. The form for delivery of that promise of a thesis depends upon the type and tone of the paper or presentation.

CONCLUDING MUSINGS

In Chapter 1 we spoke of the "trickiness" of unconcealing meaning, how these meanings emerge naturally with writing, doggedness, and determination. In this chapter we show that process of unconcealment takes on another layer, one of complicated discovery because of technology. Macrorie's "I" becomes the Internet's "I" while the "i" as self remains rooted in our search for meaning. "i" and technology merge into one act—the iSearch—an act not more difficult but faster. Thus, students are called upon to not only make connections that are valid but also to speed dial those connections. And they can if given the opportunity.

We must seem sluggish, even plodding to contemporary students who process everything more quickly than we do. Their malleable brains, exposed to technology since their neonatal period (and perhaps before), dance to a different drummer than do ours. "If children's experiences change significantly, so will their brains. Part of the brain's physical structure comes from the way it is used" (Healy, 15).

Marshall McLuhan echoes Healy, "The effects of technology do not occur at the level of opinions or concepts, rather they alter patterns of perception steadily and without any resistance" (31). Nicholas Carr, in his 2010 book *The Shallows,* re-echoes them both when he says, "The Internet, I sensed, was turning me into something like a high-speed data-processing machine, a human HAL" (16).

So here we are with our outdated, ponderous 20th century brains teaching students eagerly awaiting, for example, the new MacPro Thunderbolt 2, which doubles the speed of the old Mac. All the more reason for us to teach students to be those students who are able to discern and judge by making sense of this complex world through writing.

4 ONE TEACHER'S FORAY INTO INQUIRY BY TRAVIS LEECH

Author's Note

When we observed Travis Leech teaching middle school students in Northside ISD in San Antonio, Texas, we realized he was using the Carroll/Wilson Inquiry Schemata with some variations and adaptations. We invited Travis to write his version so readers could see the multi-dimensionality of the schemata given grade levels and purpose. To that end, we discovered we had not provided labels for each part of the schemata, so we offer them here.

The two bottom circles represent the GENERATIVE PHASE. This is ongoing from in utero with knowledge, experiences, and observations building within the brain. Writing simply taps what is there and goes on to further connections and associations.

The diamond, the GATHERING PHASE, collects in some fashion what the mind generates. Often sloppy and random, writers mine their minds for the fodder of writing. Critical because writers must discern the "wheat from the chaff."

The next circle—clearly an important phase and often a much longer one—is the PREWRITING and DRAFTING PHASE. Here student writers do what published writers do—talk, write, find, dismiss, investigate, evaluate, save, thrash.

The final circle depicts the FINISHING PHASE. With the thesis or focal point established—the promise made to the reader—the writing begins in earnest. With one eye on the audience and one eye on the purpose, writers organize, connect, and draw conclusions.

The PUBLISHING PHASE, all too often ignored, is the writer's curtain call. The piece goes public in some way—not just handed in to the teacher.

THE GENERATIVE PHASE

When setting up my unit plan for inquiry, I wanted to build on the strengths of my critical writers. As I pored over my curriculum and various resources, that all too familiar voice crept into my skull and reverberated with, "How? How will you get your kids engaged in this process?" According to Carroll & Wilson's *Acts of Teaching*, "young students begin their inquiry, as does everyone, by tapping previous knowledge, experiences, and observations" (308). Here was the "how" for my inquiry process.

I began class (I use one here as exemplar) by brainstorming issues that interested them, topics that were rolling around in their heads. I wrote their suggested topics on the white board. Here are a few examples:

- School uniforms
- Radio frequency student I.D. cards to track student attendance
- Cell phones
- Taxing foods with high fat and/or sugar

The benefit of using current topics ripped from the headlines speaks to our "now generation" of students who are constantly looking for the newest and most up-to-date trends in fashion, style, music, and culture.

I could tell things were off to a good start because the students who usually need an air horn to get out of their fog were engaged in discussion with their table group members (I have students grouped in threes or fours at tables).

Adela spoke out about using cell phones while driving because she was a passenger in a car hit by a driver who had been texting. Everyone in her group wanted to hear the story, and by the end of it decided to pursue this topic.

A boisterous group of boys livened up the back corner of the room by discussing whether or not a junk food tax was appropriate. One boy's family serves kale and tofu often, so he thought the junk food tax would help people become more aware of unhealthy eating habits. Two other boys, however, love Sonic and McDonalds now and then and didn't feel like they needed to be punished for that.

To get 12-year-olds discussing like this in class is no small feat. Yet, by writing ideas on the board and giving them choices, students easily drew upon their previous knowledge and experiences.

THE GATHERING PHASE

After this discussion based on knowledge, experiences, and observations, and after selecting topics, we moved deeper into the Carroll/Wilson Inquiry Schemata. I handed out two articles—pro and con—for each chosen topic. We spent a period reading both articles and then diving in to pull out ideas that would support each side of the topic.

Kids were critical of the ideas presented in "'Bad-Food' Taxes Will Clog Our Economic Arteries Beyond Repair" by Andrew P. Morris. One boy reacted to the author's first two sentences, "Proponents of an American Nanny State have a plan to improve your health: tax sugar and 'junk' food so you will eat less of it. Subsidies for broccoli and beets are close behind." Words flew out of his mouth as they entered his brain, but they were profound. "This guy really is letting you know right away how he feels about the junk food tax. Why isn't he trying to get people who don't agree with him on his side?"

That statement took us deeper into the article where we distinguished facts from opinions. When we dissected it, we found Morris peppered in strong opinions along with facts, skewing his article toward his side. Students who straddled the fence, or students who thought there should be no nationwide junk food tax, admitted they were turned away from the facts by his polarizing opinions. I thought, *time for a minilesson.*

"So what did we learn from this article?" I asked.

"That we need to present the facts, so people who don't agree with us can't really argue with what we say."

"Let's take that idea, and internalize it. Can we say that a persuasive writer takes other people's points of view into account when presenting a debatable idea?" I could see the light bulbs clicking on.

After evaluating and talking about the articles and finding relevant ideas that fit on both sides of the issue, we began setting up for debate. I realigned the tables to create two distinct sides, repositioning the chairs so students would face their opposition. Using butcher paper, I scrawled the words "I Agree" on one piece and "I Disagree" on the other piece, and stapled them on the opposite sides of the classroom.

"Tomorrow we debate," I told the class and I assigned homework. "Distinguish the ideas presented on both sides of the topic, add more facts and opinions." Students knew then that they would have a two-sided discussion about the topic: All cell phone use while driving should be banned.

On the day of the debate, students were to sit on the side of the room that reflected their position on the topic. Expecting an almost half and half setup, I was dismayed as student after student filed over to the "I Disagree" side, including Adele. Perplexed, I shifted uncomfortably and stared at the empty "I Agree" section. I looked at Adele and raised an eyebrow. She looked at the statement and said, "I don't think many of us want drivers to text, but I don't think hands-free devices should be illegal."

That unleashed a flood of voices. "My mom plugs her phone into her car and can talk through the speakers in her phone."

"Yeah Mr. Leech, almost all the new cars have Bluetooth for phones."

"What about if you are a passenger? I love playing games while my dad drives!"

"Is there any way we can change what's on the white board?"

Understanding a one-sided debate would be pointless, we reformulated our focus statement so there would be a more divided class. One of my brilliant introverts posed this thought, "Let's just change it to say 'All cell phone use, *except for hands free devices, should be illegal to use while driving.*'" After that revision, the class shifted into an almost perfect divide. Because of their appropriate reconstruction of the thesis statement, students were able to connect it to their thinking in fruitful debate.

In the explanation of the debate's ground rules I wanted to move them beyond what we all knew as the basics from the articles. "If you want to use facts we found in our articles, that is fine, but remember what we said about facts (the class mumbled 'they are stronger than opinions'). My challenge is to take it a step further. Try to draw a conclusion based on your facts, or tell why a particular fact makes your side of the topic stronger." I asked the students to take shorthand notes so they could reference what anyone said to support or to rebut.

One group had the most heated debate over the United States imposing a tax on fatty and sugary foods. A quiet and contemplative girl made a profound connection between people's choices to eat and drink junk food and the health risks they incur. She explained the effects of Type 2 diabetes, taking the article deeper and connecting it to the disease. Then, she put an exclamation point on her speech. "Here is the point, Type 2 diabetes happens because of the choices we make. It's the choice of whether or not to eat junk food." Her smile shown through proudly as she sat down and the kids on her side tried to stifle their shouts of approval. She high-fived a student seated next to her, and I thought the opposition would be silenced.

But the awkward silence was pierced by the most unlikely of characters, my most reluctant student. He studied his notes, and his hand shot up in the air. The boy who has trouble writing more than a few statements in connection to anything began by referencing the U.S. Constitution. He spoke about the idea that the Constitution guarantees all citizens the right to "Life, Liberty, and the Pursuit of Happiness." He talked about how he enjoyed having a soda or some candy once in a while, so he didn't see the need to punish people who eat unhealthy food in moderation, "doing what makes us happy." He of course smiled and folded his arms in a defiant, one-upped pose.

Before students went on their individual inquiry journeys, I wanted them to reflect on how powerful the previous day's debates were, and what made them so powerful. By the time kids came to me the next day, they had already learned other things about life; I wanted to bring their thinking back to how to persuade someone. I asked them to review their notes, and then answer the following questions as honestly as possible:

1. Was there a frustrating part to this exercise? If so, what was it?
2. What was the most successful portion of the exercise?
3. What was said that either caused you to change your seat (switch sides) or not change your seat (stay on your side)?
4. What conclusions can you draw about how you form your beliefs?

THE PREWRITING AND DRAFTING PHASE

Table groups shared their ideas. Through this critical thinking process, students began to understand why the debates were so powerful for everyone involved, and how they connected to writing a persuasive essay. The next appropriate step was to get them moving toward finding their own voice within a topic that interested them. Because my school subscribes to ProQuest, we had information at our fingertips covering hundreds of classic issues from abortion and school uniforms to updated issues such as cell phones and cyberbullying—all presented in student-friendly ways.

In my first year as a teacher I remember bringing my students to the computer lab, introducing all of the ProQuest articles, and then somehow ending my day in the fetal position in a dark corner of my apartment lamenting how terrible it went. With hundreds of issues, each containing at least six current newspaper or journal articles connecting to each issue, seventh-grade minds quickly went into overload, followed abruptly by disinterest or apathy toward the entire project.

The veteran version of myself wanted students to critically examine their choices before selecting a research topic. We spent a class period with a list of topics in front of us. I requested they read through the topics with a highlighter in hand, highlighting topics of high interest to them. Approximately five seconds into this activity, we encountered an issue I knew we would face. One girl's hand shot up as she read through the alphabetical topic list. "Is abortion a topic we can choose?" I was about to take the reins on a discussion about topic, when another student asked, "What is binge drinking Mr. Leech?"

"Let's think about how old we are right now, and what issues are important in our lives. Let's also think about what we want to become experts on, so we can present and maybe defend our ideas in an intelligent way. This database is one that middle and high school students can access, so there are some topics that may be more appropriate for us, and some that may be more controversial and above our maturity level. Why don't you speak with the people at your table about some of the ideas you think might be controversial, and decide whether or not seventh-grade students should become experts on these subjects, or if it is more appropriate to wait until you are a high schooler."

With that hurdle jumped and a classroom filled with kids interested in inquiring about a plethora of topics, we went to the computer lab in order to investigate and whittle down the list to a reasonable number. Students were off to the races. They needed to find articles that connected to their topics, which is a pretty easy task. Students just had to click on the topic, and they were linked to a whole host of information, including a brief overview, perhaps an explanatory video, and at least three articles that looked at both sides of the topic. After students found the article that fit their needs, they were to read it and critically analyze it.

The critical analysis focused on a series of evaluative questions:

1. Write down the title, author, and source of the article you read.
2. What is this article about?
3. What is the author's strongest idea on this topic?
4. Can you use from this article to help you write your persuasive essay? If so, what can you use?

After two quiet days of reading, our inquiry revolved around students talking about their findings. Tasked with talking in pairs for the entire class period, they took turns talking to their partner about their chosen topics. If partners had any topics in common, they discussed their findings and article evaluations with each other first. If there were no common connections, then each student shared with the partner the topic they were most likely to choose for their persuasive essay. They discussed the article or articles they read connected to that topic, shook hands, thanked their partner, and moved on to share with another classmate.

I began the next class period with a "Status of the Class" to determine their selection of research topic and the position they would be supporting. As the students shared, I made notes next to each of their names on the class roster.

Students chose issues from the ethics of young girls in beauty pageants to Lance Armstrong's story of coming clean about taking performance-enhancing drugs during his *Tour De France* racing days. They took positions on cyberbullying, children under 18 using tanning salons, whether or not students should have the choice to complete school online, and the positive effects of youth sports outweighing youth injuries, among others.

THE FINISHING PHASE

I wanted my classes to have a chance to organize their data as they began the writing process. While in the computer lab, students had printed off copies of articles that supported their positions on the topic and articles opposing them. Students had read the articles, but I assumed the data in their minds were still pretty raw and absorbed only at a surface level.

This became a segue into organizing by using a T-Chart that housed their positions, along with the top supporting and opposing arguments. This way, students knew they had the support they needed to reference in their essay, and the support they wanted to use was available to quote from reliable sources.

Constructing a thesis statement is the make or break moment for any persuasive essay. I modeled a series of theses statements, good and bad, to show how a thesis statement can be revised to properly help a reader know the point of an essay.

We practiced this. I invited students to sacrifice their theses statements to the writing gods so we could analyze and revise (or not) them as a class.

With the students, now equipped with a working thesis and most already enlightened enough to write their introductory paragraph, I moved to Kenneth Bruffee's four main types of essay formats (28–37; 78–81; 82–83; 84–85; 86–87; also in Carroll & Wilson, 60–61).

Turning on the doc camera, I projected my model persuasive essay. Each paragraph was written on an individual notecard: one introduction, two pro arguments, two con arguments, and a conclusion. I spent the next chunk of class time modeling how to rearrange my paragraph cards to fit each of different organizational patterns.

With sticky notes in hand, and approaching Bruffee's patterns one by one, students suggested transitional sentences I could stick onto my notecards. With this modeling and the information they had collected, by the end of class they understood how easy it would be to choose a pattern that matched their meaning. They also realized they didn't need to rewrite or redraft their essays or change their argumentative approach. This now made them fearless to grab notecards and begin writing. The modeling worked.

MARY BETH AS EXEMPLAR

Mary Beth used the first drafting day to furiously fill six notecards with information. She referred to her articles often, highlighting information she was going to quote in her essay. The most surprising aspect of Mary Beth's essay is that the writing took on another persona, one totally foreign to her classroom manner.

While explaining each of Bruffee's argument essay patterns, I introduced Strawman as something a prosecuting attorney may use. This pattern gives enough information about the opposition to entice the reader, right before the author destroys the opposition's credibility. When the writer then swoops in with the strongest reason of support and wham, persuasion happens. I cautioned them that this pattern could be tricky because they would be attacking the other side, which may alienate the reader.

I brought this up to Mary Beth in conference, wondering aloud why she wanted to go on the offensive. She told me straight away about her thoughts on what true beauty is for girls. It is what you do and who you are, not how you look. I came away from that conversation pleased she could put her true feelings down on paper in a way that didn't compromise who she was.

Below is Mary Beth's first draft on notecards (fig. 4.1). She began her essay by connecting to previous knowledge about the television show *Toddlers and Tiaras,* which she had seen multiple times. This connection happened organically for Mary Beth.

Drafting was a complete success because students had a clear understanding of their topic and a clear framework of how to present it in writing. Within the confines of revision, I made sure students

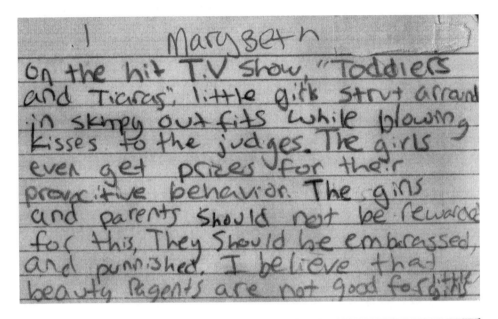

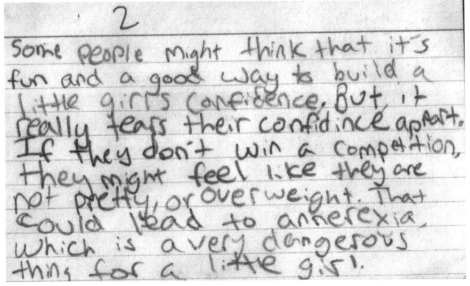

Figure 4.1. Mary Beth's Notecards

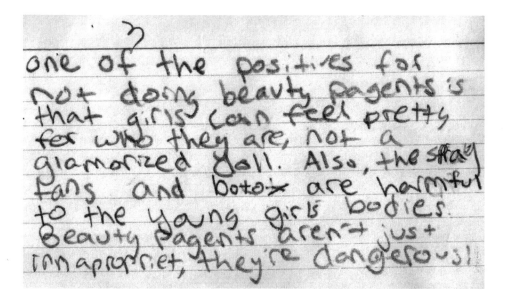

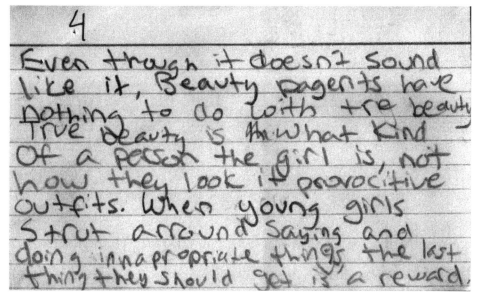

Figure 4.1. *(Continued)*

incorporated connections to previous knowledge or experiences and were able to draw appropriate conclusions that fit with their side of the argument.

Peer revision is something that was built into our class throughout the year. We began with "Say Back" (Carroll & Wilson, 75). Students took turns reading and writing as I popped in on various groups and listened, jotting down sticky note ideas for one or two people per table. My hope for "Say Back" was that these young writers would realize they did some positive things in their first draft, making them more willing to go back into their next draft to make it better.

Day two of revision found the class diving into each other's essays to look for connections. Students needed to critically examine each other's essays to look for examples of connections to personal experience that gave the author credibility, or connections to prior knowledge—the articles they read during the prewriting phase.

Again I began by modeling. I used purple and blue highlighters to color the connections I had made in my essay. When I connected to the personal experience, I highlighted in purple. When I connected to an article, I used blue.

Students did the same. They used purple highlighters for personal experience connections and blue highlighters for prior knowledge connections. In the meantime, I met with students individually to conference about their progress and goals for the second draft.

When second drafts were completed, we needed to do a final smoothing out of the essay to make it fit the formal tone of an argumentative essay. For this to happen, one class period was spent using Carroll's strategy of ratiocination. This technique allows students to "manipulate sentences, consider syntax and diction, . . . develop and clarify their thinking, and revise their writing" (Carroll & Wilson,120). My critical writers worried about the format of their essays and the strength of their arguments, but they had yet to dive into the nuts and bolts of their writing to make sure it captured their true voices and made sense for others. That brought us to ratiocination.

Below is Mary Beth's ratiocinated second draft. She clearly understands the meaning behind the different colors and symbols that enable her to think deeply about what she had written—the very word *ratiocination* means a process of logical thought or reason (fig. 4.2).

Upon completion of ratiocination, we went to the computer lab and used two more class periods to type up our final drafts. Students had clear instructions to guide them in creating a final draft with a formal tone, filled with appropriate connections to life

By Mary Beth

Beauty Pageants

On hit T.V show *Toddlers and Tiaras*, Little girls scream, shout and pout at their parents. They dress up in skimpy outfits and blow kisses to the judges. They even get prizes for their provocative behavior. It may be surprising, but this is the real life of beauty pageant families. The little girls shouldn't be rewarded for the horrible things they do! They should instead be embarrassed and punished. I believe that beauty pageants are not appropriate for little girls to participate in.

Some people might think that it's fun, and a good way to build little girl's confidence. However it really tears their confidence apart. If they don't win a competition, they might feel like they are not pretty enough, or overweight. That could lead to anorexia, which is a very dangerous thing for anyone! Also, according to Melinda Tankard Reist, "Pageants encourage us to see little girls as older than they really are which is a dangerous thing to do."

One of the positives for not doing beauty pageants if that girls can feel pretty for whom they are, not a glamorized doll. Also, spray tans

Figure 4.2. Mary Beth's Ratiocination

By Mary Beth

and Botox are harmful to the young girl's bodies. Beauty pageants

aren't just inappropriate, they're dangerous.

Even though it doesn't sound like it, beauty pageants have nothing to

do with true beauty. True beauty is what kind a person the girl is, not

how they look in provocative outfits. Parents who let their children

participate in beauty pageants should be embarrassed, and

ashamed.

Figure 4.2. *(Continued)*

Mary Beth

Beauty Pageants

On hit TV show <u>Toddlers and Tiaras</u>, little girls scream, shout and pout at their parents. They dress up in skimpy outfits and blow kisses to the judges. They even receive prizes for their provocative behavior! It may be surprising, but this is the real life of beauty pageant families. The young girls shouldn't be rewarded for the horrible things they do! The whole idea of a competition of "beauty" is ludicrous! Little girls should not be allowed to participate in beauty pageants.

Some people might think that it's fun, and a good way to build little girl's confidence. However it really tears their confidence apart. If they don't win a competition, they might feel like they're not pretty enough, or overweight. That could lead to anorexia, which is a very dangerous thing for anyone! Also, according to Melinda Tankard Reist, "Pageants encourage us to see little girls as older than they really are which is a dangerous thing to do."

One of the positives for not doing beauty pageants is that girls can feel pretty for whom they are, not a glamorized doll. Also, spray tans and Botox are harmful to the young girl's bodies. Beauty pageants aren't just inappropriate, they're dangerous.

Even though it doesn't sound like it, beauty pageants have nothing to do with true beauty. True beauty is what kind of person the girl is, not how they look in provocative outfits. Parents who let their children participate in beauty pageants should feel embarrassed, and ashamed. That would be fine.

Figure 4.3. Mary Beth's Finished Piece

experiences and published articles. Here is Mary Beth's final piece and here it is published (fig. 4.3)!

CONCLUDING MUSINGS

Everyone in education knows how tough teaching middle school can be, especially seventh grade, so we were delighted to see how engaged Leech's students became with inquiry. Choice played a big part in the enthusiasm, as did Leech's own energy—but as V. S. Ramachandran says, "The brain, like nature, abhors a vacuum" (4). Obviously Leech filled those brains with possibilities and once the students realized the intellectual fun they could have, they were as Leech says, "off and running."

That the inquiry process mirrors the writing process, that writers—no matter their ages—backtrack and move forward in their search for truth, which underscored the work of these adolescents. Most impressive, for example, is Mary Beth's revision of her thesis. Nestled between two stars on her ratiocinated notecards, Mary Beth wrote the quintessential awkward sentence, "I believe that beauty pageants are not appropriate for little girls to participate in." In earlier times this would have earned her a big read AWK. But with ratiocination and the process in full swing, she honed that sentence into a much more powerful, clearer, and direct thesis statement, "Little girls should not be allowed to participate in beauty pageants." She makes her assertion and she states it well. Realizing how much better *she* made her writing will help Mary Beth think of herself more and more often as a writer. She knows something about herself she didn't know before the query process.

Reading between the lines of Leech's foray into query, it becomes clear that seventh-graders use talk as their impetus. Leech allows for that. Even though "talk" appears in the schemata during the prewriting/drafting phase, he, as the savvy teacher, encourages it throughout the process. By orchestrating their verbal acknowledgments, their adolescent angst, their tentative tiptoes into inquiry, his students become confident about what they want to say and how they want to say it. This, in turn, will embolden and catapult them up the happy scale of gleaning some heretofore unnoticed bit and thereby learning through that unconcealment.

> All great works of literature either dissolve a genre or invent one.
>
> —Walter Benjamin

 # FOUR UNIQUE VIEWS OF INQUIRY AND A NEW FORM

MULTIPLE GENRES

"Papa" Romano

If Janet Emig is the ordained "mama" of process, then Tom Romano is the official "papa" of blending genres. We heard him at NCTE and invited him to speak in 1997 at our 11th Annual Abydos Trainers' and Teachers' Conference in Austin, Texas.

The first time he wowed us with his story of how Michael Ondaatje's *The Collected Works of Billy the Kid* (1970) fascinated and inspired him. The second time we heard how that inspiration turned into his concept of multigenre research.

Certainly those of us who taught in the 1960s were doing some integrating of genres (remember collages?) and in the 1970s Emig invited us to project through geometric renderings, song, poetry, even drama and dance our honed individual definitions of writing as a process. But these were dalliances until Romano wrote *Writing with Passion: Life Stories, Multiple Genres.* There he explained and convinced how much deeper learning would be if we melded facts, interpretation, and imagination. He held in 1995 that "each genre offers me ways of seeing and understanding that others do not. I perceive the world through multiple genres. They shape my seeing. They define who I am" (109).

I, for one, needed little convincing because what flashed through my mind was a college course entitled "Art, Music, and Literature." I loved that course. We studied "periods" in the arts via the art, music, and literature of each period.

As we entered "Impressionism," I became lost in the definitions of objectifying reality, and transitory mental images, so understanding eluded me—until the professor played Claude Debussy's *Prelude to the Afternoon of a Faune.* Not being particularly musical (I play no musical instrument—much to my personal disappointment) and know little about metrical pulse and orchestral timbres (even being slightly hard of hearing), I listened to Debussy's symphonic poem and totally understood Impressionism.

Was it because I had seen the art and read the literature first? Had I internalized the characteristics of the movement? Was it something suggested but not quite obvious in the music? Was it what I could hear? Whatever, that memory connected to what Romano said, and I understood when he explained how each genre is a different way of "seeing."

Melding Multigenres and Inquiry

Peter Allen wrote a wonderfully joyful title "Everything Old Is New Again" for the great film *All That Jazz,* directed by Bob Fosse. That title encapsulates multigenres. Like a planet, each genre has a life in its own universe, but when pulled out and placed side by side another planet in a different part of the universe, it holds a different meaning. The old becomes new again. And "what had been hiding . . . for centuries crawled out." Sometime in the second century B.C., Terence said, "There's nothing to say that hasn't been said before" (Shields, 7). That Terence was on to something!

By now anyone who reads knows how the neurons in our brains make connections. That is their business. That is how we know. Further, the more connections those neurons make, the more they *can* make because those cells change every time we experience or observe something new. They grow longer or fatter dendrites, or they grow more of those little "twigs." (Under a high-powered microscope, neurons look like branches and dendrites look like twigs. Even in this discovery, connections were made!) So the old adage, "The more you know the more you can know," finds supportive roots in brain research.

We offer this syllogism: If inquiry is the seeking out of information, as we suggest in Chapter 2, then what better way to discover relationships and connections (and grow dendrites) than by juxtaposing the known with something similar, thereby enacting one of the first phases in Vygotsky's concept development. Side by side the second piece looks different, takes on a different meaning—not new necessarily—but different.

And if "[i]nquiry is an approach to learning whereby students find and use a variety of sources of information and ideas to increase their understanding of a problem, topic, or issue." If "it requires more of them than simply answering questions or getting a right answer." If "it espouses investigation, exploration, search, quest, research, pursuit, and study." And if it "does not stand alone, but it engages, interests, and challenges students to connect their world with the curriculum" (Kuhlthau, Maniotes, & Caspari, 2) then it stands to reason a form not unlike multigenre would rise up around it.

Shields in his manifesto reminds us that "[e]very artistic movement from the beginning of time is an attempt to figure out a way to smuggle more of what the artist thinks is reality into the work of art" (3). Further, he suggests using "a multitude of forms and media—lyric essay, prose poem, collage novel, visual art, film, television, radio, performance art, rap, stand-up comedy, graffiti" (3), each characterized by "randomness, openness to accident and serendipity, spontaneity, artistic risk, emotional urgency and intensity, reader/viewer participation, an overly literal tone, plasticity of form, pointillism, criticism as autobiography, self-reflexivity, self-ethnography, anthropological autobiography, a blurring of any distinction between fiction and nonfiction: the lure and blur of the real" (5) brings new meanings. "Everything old is new again." In a word—organic; in short—a new genre—a multigenre that matches the simultaneous literacy of the 21st century.

The historical "straw binaries" (Ingham, 15) of fiction and nonfiction explode within contemporary writing that includes fables of fact, the nonfiction novel, creative nonfiction, presentational literature, symbolic action, experimental fiction, slam poetry, memoir vs monologue, multigenerational sagas, and even books like David Shields's *Reality Hunger: A Manifesto* that defy placement in a single form.

This literary montage is not for the pinch-minded, but it is for the open-minded who in expressing their findings want the freedom of repetend and assemblage. That would be—in this case—students.

Corita Kent, the educator and artist known for her vibrant serigraphs, held to 10 rules. Rule 6 applies here: "Nothing is a mistake. There's no win and no fail. There's only make" (176). Her rule fits the multigenre paper—the mistakes of typical papers are anathema; with the multigenre inquiry there is only *imaginción.* There is only *conexión.*

APPLICATIONS OF THE C/W INQUIRY SCHEMATA

Teachers in an Institute

Melinda Clark as an Abydos trainer applied the Carroll/Wilson Inquiry Schemata during her training of teachers. In doing so, she put a twist on the schemata by enlarging it and engaging the participants visually and kinetically. Following is her description of what happened:

The Value of the Authentic Inquiry by Melinda Clark

While I value authentic inquiry, I never totally understood how to use the Carroll/Wilson Inquiry Schemata in the classroom. I taught my first three-week institute this summer and struggled with the day ten lesson on the inquiry schemata. I had to find a way for teachers to share ownership in the research process. Debbie Gerth, my co-presenter, savior, and mentor those three weeks, suggested that I follow what Becky Stortz, another Abydos Trainer, did the previous summer. I knew Debbie would never steer me wrong but still had misgivings about my whole understanding of the lesson and conveying its significance to teachers.

Following Debbie's suggestion, I set out on a scavenger hunt to gather items large enough to trace and construct life-size inquiry schemata. Using a trashcan for a circle and a large picture book for the diamond, I rolled out six feet of butcher paper. After tracing the shapes on the page, I labeled it, drew in all the recursive arrows, and hung it on a column in the library. As participants entered the library the following morning, I handed them each a sticky note and asked them to write their name on it.

We discussed the importance of inquiry-based learning and conducting research as a process. Participants pointed out that many of their extensive pieces—expository/research essays emerged from the inquiry that occurred while prewriting for their reflexive (personal narrative) pieces. Surprisingly, adults just like students doubt themselves as experts. Discussing the inquiry schemata and focusing on the recursive nature of the research process reinforced what participants already knew; most needed to do more questioning and exploring.

After nudging the participants to dig deeper into their prior knowledge, we moved our discussion over to the life-sized inquiry schemata. I asked participants to identify where they were on the inquiry schemata and place their sticky note accordingly. During our in-depth conversation about where each person was on the inquiry schemata, participants intermittently moved their sticky notes up or down showing the truly recursive nature of research and inquiry.

I believed that my lesson ended with the placement of the sticky notes. To my surprise, participants continued to utilize the inquiry schemata. By the end of day ten, most of the sticky notes had been moved at least once. On day eleven, participants entered the library and went straight for the inquiry schemata. Some, frustratingly, slapped their sticky notes from the prewriting stage back to the note taking stage. Others breathed a sigh of relief as they moved their sticky notes from the prewriting stage to the actual writing stage.

Participants further up the schemata found themselves as resources for those still struggling to climb into the writing phase. The collaboration between participants became a visual representation of Vygotsky's Zone of Proximal Development (250) as those further along in the process assisted in moving their colleagues up the schemata.

As Debbie and I observed the participants utilizing the inquiry schemata to track their own progress, we realized we were looking at a life-size status of the class. Atwell, who credits Graves for the idea (38), conducted status of the class through class discussion. We used the visual to determine who needed additional conferencing. Participants commented that the visual and kinetic nature of the life-size inquiry schemata cemented in their minds the importance of moving through the inquiry process and circling back until they better understood their topics.

Stortz's adaptation of the Wilson/Carroll Inquiry Schemata resulted in aha! moments for the participants and for me. The idea of having students move their own sticky notes as they journeyed through the research process excited me. After teaching my first three-week institute, many of the lessons came alive for me. I applaud Carroll and Wilson for designing a "model for inquiry applicable for all grade levels with allowances made for time, topic, and diversification" (308). I'm eager to construct a new life-size inquiry schemata, laminate it, and staple it to my wall. I'm confident my students will experience a newfound excitement for inquiry just as I did.

Third Graders

Lori Maldonado, a participant in the institute, took the notion of the C/W Inquiry Schemata and worked it into her third-grade curriculum. She, too, wrote about the experience and the results. Following is her description of what happened:

Inquiry: Where Do I Go from Here? by Lori Michelle Maldonado

I teach third graders, so questions come as naturally to them as hugs. As a consequence, inquiry happens naturally, and daily, in my classroom. There is always a discussion happening about where something came from or why something works the way it does. Often inquiry is addressed in a simple conversation with a student.

"Why do you think Benjamin Franklin made his flippers out of wood Mrs. Maldonado?" one student asked me last year.

"I do not know, but I am curious. Where do you think you could find the answer to that question?"

"Probably on Google" was his response, typical of kids from this technology-driven generation.

"Probably. Any other thoughts?" I asked, to which he just shrugged.

"I wonder if the library has any books on Benjamin Franklin and his inventions." I posed.

Sure enough, about a week later, that student showed up to class with a book he had checked out from the library and a few pages he had printed from the Internet. He was so excited to share his findings with me, and I was excited to share his inquiry process with the class.

Other times a question posed in class allows the entire class to participate in the inquiry process. Once, while reading *Pop's Bridge* by Eve Bunting, a student asked if the Golden Gate Bridge was real. When I answered yes and pulled up a map of the San Francisco area on my computer to show them the actual location and photographs, the onslaught of curiosity began.

"Is it really that long?"

"Did men really hang up there like in the story to build it?"

"Did some men really die while building that bridge?"

They couldn't get the questions out fast enough. I had my lesson plan prepared; we were supposed to be discussing cause and effect that day. But that would have to wait as a better lesson had just presented itself. It was the proverbial teachable moment!

A discussion of possible sources to find the answers to their questions followed, and pretty soon I had kids on the computer, a few in the library looking for books, and a couple more down the hall interviewing a teacher who had visited San Francisco that summer. The kids devoured every bit of information they could find about the Golden Gate Bridge and when we reread the story later that week, their deep comprehension of the story, from the setting to the characters, was amazing. I never taught that lesson on cause and effect but not one student failed the test I gave on *Pop's Bridge*. Proof of how amazingly powerful inquiry can be.

There comes a time during the course of the year that my third graders need to produce an inquiry paper on their own. They are free to choose the topic; I want them to be passionate about it. Atwell says choice creates ownership, Carroll says choice equals voice; it makes students more engaged in their writing. Assigning students a topic to research is a fruitless as choosing a memory for them to write a personal narrative about.

Through a variety of prewriting activities, I assist students in narrowing their topics. Carroll and Wilson, in their book *Acts of Teaching*, suggest prewriting activities such as sentence stubs, listing, and looping. Then the students create an "Inquiry Box" from a Kleenex box, shoe box, cereal box, or a plain brown paper bag. This "Inquiry Box," also from the brilliant minds of Carroll and Wilson in *Acts of Teaching*, becomes "home" to note cards with information learned or sketches drawn, tidbits cut from magazines, copies of things printed from the Internet, and lists of questions to explore. Just as I allowed them to choose their inquiry topic, I allow them to make "guided decisions" about where to do their research. I say "guided decisions" because I do not want students to only use the Internet or think they can only read books on their topic. I act as a facilitator, and sometimes as a source, as students begin the inquiry process.

Several days are dedicated to answering those burning questions, organizing information, and possibly even drafting their findings before I intervene. My intervention is purposefully timed. I place a large copy of the Carroll/Wilson Inquiry Schemata, from *The Acts of Teaching* (309), drawn out on butcher paper on the floor and the students gather around. I ask the students to read me some of the words they see on the schemata, and we discuss their meaning and their role in the inquiry process. I ask students if any of them used personal experiences or prior knowledge in their research and invite them to share. We talk about the different ways we take notes, and I have students who have identified unique sources share. We talk about each step on the schemata, following the arrows up. Then I pose a scenario to the students allowing them practice using the schemata.

Scenario one: "Lori has been to the lake near her home many times and has seen warning signs about harmful bacteria in the water. She has noticed that very few people swim in the lake. Lori is curious about what the bacterium is and where it is coming from. She has decided to call the City Parks Department to see what she can find out. Where is she on the Inquiry Schemata?"

Before answering the question about where "Lori" is in the inquiry process, we walk through where she has been. *I actually walk on the schemata* as the students point out what parts of the inquiry process "Lori" has already been through and we eventually come to where she is now. My next question for the students is where "Lori" can go next. Together we examine the Inquiry Schemata and students share their ideas for the next step. I then give the students another scenario and have a volunteer walk on the schemata while the others help to direct them.

Scenario two: "Julie has been researching the evolution of exercise. She has been to the library and done some research online. She also went to her gym and interviewed a personal trainer. She has done some prewriting but doesn't feel she has enough information for a thorough report. Where is she on the Inquiry Schemata?"

Together we discover where "Julie" has been on the schemata and discuss how she is writing now but doesn't feel like she has enough information to write a thorough report on exercise. So I ask the students what she can do next. Using this scenario, students can visually see that "Julie" may have to go backward in the process as the volunteer student walks backward on the poster. Even though she's already at the writing stage, she will have to go back and collect more information.

I have two additional scenarios that I use and again I have the students walk on the schemata as I read, and we discuss the Inquiry Process in a very deep and meaningful way.

Scenario three: "Eddie has been searching for a topic to research. He made a list of topics that he has some knowledge about or is interested in. Where is he on the Inquiry Schemata?"

Scenario four: "Joyce discovered while writing her personal narrative about her new puppy that she was very interested in the topic of puppy care. In particular she wanted to know more about the shots puppies need and why. She interviewed her vet and read some information the vet gave her. Joyce also did some research online. She's almost done with her puppy how-to and thinks others may be interested in reading it, especially if they are considering getting a puppy. Where is she on the Inquiry Schemata?"

After the discussion of the four scenarios, I take the students into their writing and ask them to think about where they are in the process. Then I ask them to go stand on the Inquiry Schemata at the point they think they are currently at. With a partner nearby, preferably at the same stage, I encourage students to talk to each other about where they are in the inquiry process and where they could go next. I ask the partner to listen respectfully so that they can make suggestions of different sources or ideas as I walk through the groups offering assistance as needed. This is Vygotsky's zone of proximal development (ZPD) hard at work. Through this collaborative discussion, more capable writers assist less capable students, and the teacher acts as resource when needed. "Using the zone of proximal development as an educational tool serves us well when teaching the writing process" (Carroll and Wilson, 250).

From here the inquiry process continues as students collect data, prewrite, and finally draft their findings. Now each day before starting writer's workshop to work on our inquiry papers, I ask the students to go stand on the Inquiry Schemata to show me where they are, a virtual "status of the class" (Atwell), allowing me to quickly determine who needs my intervention in the form of a conference that day.

Like all writing, inquiry is recursive and using the Carroll and Wilson Inquiry Schemata this way makes this come alive for students. The application of this process to other genres of writing becomes natural.

Acknowledgments

I'd like to thank Dr. Carroll and Mr. Wilson for allowing me the opportunity to be a part of their book. I never considered myself a writer but Abydos changed that. Thank you to my husband Vann and my M&Ms (Maxx and Milo) for allowing me the time to devote to this project. A special thank you to my colleagues who read and edited my writing, offered ideas or suggestions, or just listened to me talk through the process—Kristen Johnson, Georgia Edwards, Alyshea Techam, and Julie Schweers. Your support means the world to me!

A YEAR-LONG APPROACH TO INQUIRY

Kim Bailey, an Abydos trainer from Aldine ISD, recently presented a professional staff development session on "Practicing the Authentic Inquiry Process—All Year Long." She began her session by quoting Wilson who always tells the trainers, "Research should not be an event."

An event in our minds happens once—maybe once in a while—and it's a big deal with trappings galore. Everyone gets geared up and much hinges on the outcome, sometimes even passing the course for the semester. Spending time on all the intricacies of THE PAPER often sends an incorrect message to students—that form, not content, matters. Plagiarism runs rampant. Districts, schools, and teachers develop all manner of machinations to circumvent "lifted" papers. Even going to the library becomes a version of solitary confinement—no talking, no peer grouping lest someone copy. No conferring with the teacher lest that someone gets an edge.

What have we done to inquiry? Have we turned it into a series of hoops to jump through instead of honoring what it is—a process of discovery?

What we know about authentic inquiry is that people who are truly interested in a subject become obsessed with it. Małgorzata Grabowski, an Abydos trainee from Donna ISD, in one of her reflections, says it this way:

> Through this training and the required readings, I realize that when I seek the answer to my question, I learn a lot more than just the answer because finding one answer leads me to more questions. I see how asking questions and engaging in inquiry can build students' background knowledge as well as a love of learning, so I am now incorporating more opportunities for inquiry in my classroom.

Even our littlest learners will remain engrossed in a subject that matters to them. My three-year-old Goddaughter (to whom this book is dedicated) will spend hours sorting and examining seashells but will hardly glance at a doll. She watches the YouTube video of "High-Diving Giraffes" repeatedly, laughing at the one who licks at the camera with his purple tongue and squealing as they dive again and again into the water. She wants books on giraffes; she creates "giraffes" when she writes; she talks about the time she fed the giraffe in the Houston Zoo some lettuce. At three she is already a true inquirer. True inquirers will ferret out books and articles on the subject, remain on the Internet for hours following leads, skimming and scanning, looking and discovering, reading and talking and learning. And when they unconceal something they didn't know, all those neurons fire up, giving a pleasurable feeling, one we call "satisfaction." Therein lies the excitement of true inquiry.

So when Bailey said in her presentation, "Inquiry should be an authentic and on-going process," we were all ears. How did this authentic inquiry happen in Aldine, a huge district, 66th in the nation, 9th in Texas? But size did not deter Aldine—or Bailey.

The origin of a year-long inquiry born of Wilson's quote began by breaking down what Bailey calls "the C-W Inquiry Schemata" into four nine-week segments (fig. 5.1). This need for a breakdown stems from a struggle the teachers were having with gaining a true concept of what an authentic inquiry process looks like in the classroom and how it correlates to all the requirements, formats, and good pedagogy.

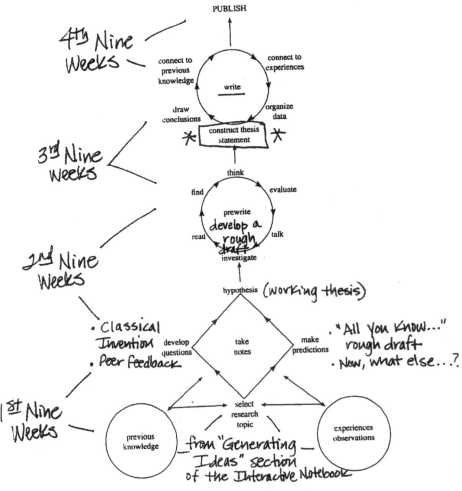

Figure 5.1. The Four Nine-Week C-W Inquiry Schemata

After this analysis, Aldine knew that the ownership of the subject of inquiry depended upon passion for that subject. So they called upon teachers to initiate what they call a Reader's/Writer's Notebook. Movement through this notebook and its sections authenticate ways that would help students through the inquiry process. Every student in Aldine ISD keeps this tabbed notebook.

The Writing Section

- Generating Ideas—the inquiry process begins here
- Conventions—(editing)
- Craft—(revising)
- Word Study—(word parts, origins, relationships, etc.)

The Reading Section

- Documentation of What I Read (requirements) Want to Read (self-selected)
- Reading Minilessons (reading skills)
- Reader Response
- Research Formalities

As an example of how this works, see Year-at-a-Glance 2013–2014 English II (fig. 5.2). Please note this year of inquiry, which includes expository, persuasive, and literary writing, culminates with a creative writing, multigenre research project.

Bailey is quick to point out that she cannot take credit for the district expectations and implementation of the notebook, but she has been successful in synthesizing all of the information—the state TEKS (Texas's variation of the Core Curriculum), the writing process, classroom syllabi, and lesson plans so that teachers see how authentic reading and writing (specifically inquiry) are practiced in a real-world, integrated way (figs. 5.3 and 5.4). It was she who suggested the Carroll/Wilson Schemata as its bare bones outline. We should note that although this curriculum is currently being used in the district, it is in various stages of implementation at different schools across the district and is considered at all time to be work in progress. This, too, is a process.

Year at a Glance 2013–2014

English I

	1st Semester		2nd Semester	
	1st Nine Weeks Aug. 26–Oct. 25, 2013	2nd Nine Weeks Oct. 28–Jan. 16, 2014	3rd Nine Weeks Jan. 21–Mar. 28, 2014	4th Nine Weeks Mar. 31–June 5, 2014
ASSESSMENT	**Process Piece—Literary** **Diag 1&2 Aug. 26–Sept. 13** Timed Writing Diagnostic: Expository and Literary **Test 1 Oct. 7–11** District Timed Writing: Literary	**Process Piece—** Expository **Test 2 Jan. 6–10** District Timed Writing: Expository **Test 3 Jan. 13–16** Benchmark: Revising & Editing Reading/ Literary Analysis 2 Short Answer	**Process Piece—** Literary or Expository (at Teacher's Discretion) **Test 4 Mar. 17–21** District Timed Writing: Expository NOTE: TEKS covered this 9 week are at teacher's discretion based on student's needs.	**Process Piece—** Persuasive/Research Paper **STAAR English I EOC** **Test 5: PBA (Persuasive Research Paper)**–Due in Eduphoria by May 23 **Test 6 May 19–23** District Timed Writing: Persuasive
WORD STUDY	1A–Technical/Academic Meaning 1B–Analyze Textual Context & Connotation 1E–Dictionary, Glossary, and Thesaurus Use	1A–Roots and affixes 1E–Etymology	1C–Analogies 1D–Origins and meanings of foreign words and phrases	**Review All**

READING MINI-LESSONS	RCA–Comprehension RCB–Inferences 2–Theme and Genre 3–Poetry 4–Drama 5–Fiction 7–Sensory Language 12–Media	RCA–Comprehension RCB–Inferences 8–Culture and History 9–Expository Text 11–Procedural Text 12–Media	RCA–Comprehension RCB–Inferences 2–Theme and Genre 3–Poetry 4–Drama 5–Fiction 7–Sensory Language 8–Culture and History 9–Expository Text 10–Persuasive Text 11–Procedural Text 12–Media	RCA–Comprehension RCB–Inferences 2–Theme and Genre 4–Drama 10–Persuasive Text
WRITING CRAFT	13–Writing (Process) 14–Literary Writing	13–Writing (Process) 15–Expository and Procedural Review of Previous TEKS as Needed	**See 1st and 2nd Nine Weeks**	13–Writing (Process) 15–Multi-Media
WRITING CONVENTIONS	17–Conventions (Parts of Speech, Sentence Structure) 18–Mechanics (Capitalization) 19–Spellings	17–Conventions (Tenses and Clauses) 18–Mechanics (Punctuation) Review of Previous TEKS as Needed	22B–Sources 22C–Critique Research Process	17–Conventions (Subjunctive Mood, Sentence Variety) 18–Mechanics Review of Previous TEKS as Needed
RESEARCH PROCESS	20–Generate Research Ideas 21–Planning 23–MLA	22A–Focus and Evaluation of topic		23–Organization – Focus and Coherence-Evaluation
	TEKS 24, 25, and 26 (Listening, Speaking & Teamwork) are to be taught and reinforced throughout the entire school year.			

Figure 5.2. Year-at-a-Glance

Continuum of Research Skills and Requirements for Performance-Based Assessment
Grades 9–10

	Research Product	Objective	Length	Number of Teacher-Approved Sources	Source Type
9th	Documented Persuasive Essay with oral presentation and additional related projects(s)	Students will advocate a position and support their opinion through the research process. Students will produce a research project that includes a documented persuasive essay, oral presentation, and additional related project. 9.16 (A–E) 9.25 (A)	3–5 pages typed not including bibliography, coversheet, and any visual aids. 2–3 minute oral presentation 9.23 (E) 9.25 (A)	4 or more Aldine district resources (variety of sources) Internet resources (reliable) LMC reference materials 9.22 (B) 9.21 (B–C) 8.23 (D)	Primary and Secondary
10th	Documented Persuasive Essay with oral presentation, visual aides, and additional related project(s)	Students will advocate a position and support their opinion through the research process. Students will produce a research project that includes a documented persuasive essay, oral presentation, and additional related project. 10.16 (A–F) 10.25 (A)	3–5 pages typed not including bibliography, coversheet, and any visual aids. 3–5 minute oral presentation 10.23 (E) 10.25 (A)	5 or more district resources (variety of sources) Internet resources (reliable) LMC reference materials 10.22 (B) 10.21 (B–C) 8.23 (D)	Primary and Secondary

• **Integrate writing requirements with research products**

High School Language Arts_Revised_Summer 2013

Figure 5.3. Continuum of Research Skills, Grades 9–10

Focus and Coherence	Development of Ideas (Research Conventions)	Style	Conventions	Process
Establishes a thesis that effectively states a position and clearly takes a stand. *10.16 (A)* Write a multi-paragraph persuasive essay w/appropriate org. structure. *9.16 (D)* Effective introductions and conclusions *9.15 (Ai)* Range of arguments and appeals *9.16 (B, C)* Logical transitions *9.15 (Aii)* Synthesis and analysis of information from several sources *9.16 (E)*	Integrate quotations and citations into written text *9.21 (C)* Paraphrasing and Summarizing *9.21 (C)* Synthesize/analyze Information *9.23* Relevant information/valid inferences *9.15 (Av)* Document with in-text citations *9.21 (C); 9.23 (E)*	Write a variety of complete sentences (i.e. simple, compound, complex, compound-complex) *9.17 (A–C)*	Use standard spelling, capitalization and punctuation *9.18 (A–B—includes all TEKS in strand)*	Writing Process (Pre-writing, drafting, revision, editing, conferencing, publishing *9.13 (A–E)* Source and note cards *9.21 (C); 9.23 (E)* Research Plan *9.20 (A–B)* Research Vocabulary: • works cited • citation • source • synthesize • relevance • paraphrase • plagiarism • valid • MLA
Establishes a thesis that effectively states a position and clearly takes a stand. *10.16 (A)* Write a multi-paragraph essay w/appropriate org. structure *10.16 (D)* Effective introductions and conclusions *10.15 (Ai)* Range of arguments and appeals *10.16 (B, C, F)* Logical transitions *10.15 (Aii)* Synthesis and analysis of information from several sources *10.16 (E)*	Integrate quotations and citations into written text *10.21 (C)* Paraphrasing and Summarizing *10.21 (C)* Synthesize/analyze information *10.23* Relevant information/valid inferences *10.16 (A)* Document with in-text citations *10.21 (C); 10.23 (E)*	Write a variety of complete sentences (i.e. simple, compound, complex, compound-complex) *10.17 (A–C)*	Use standard spelling, capitalization and punctuation *10.18 (A–B—includes all TEKS in strand)*	Writing Process (Pre-writing, drafting, revision, editing, conferencing, publishing *10.13 (A–E)* Source and note cards *10.21 (C); 10.23 (E)* Research Plan *10.20 (A, B); 10.21 (A); 10.22 (A, C)* Research Vocabulary: • works cited • citation • source • synthesize • relevance • paraphrase • plagiarism • validity • reliability • MLA

Continuum of Research Skills and Requirements for Performance-Based Assessment

Grades 11–12

	Research Product	Objective	Length	Number of Teacher-Approved sources	Source Type
11th	Expository Analysis Essay with oral presentation with visual slides, and additional related written and/or multimedia project(s)	Students will produce a research project that includes an expository analysis report, an oral presentation, and additional related written and/or multimedia project(s) *11.15 A* *11.20 (A–E)* *11.25 (A)*	4–6 pages typed not including bibliography, coversheet, and any graphic support **11.23 (E)** 4–5 minute oral presentation *11.25 (A)*	6 or more Aldine district resources Internet resources (reliable) LMC reference materials *11.21 (B–C)* *11.22 (B)* *8.23 (D)*	Primary and Secondary
12th	Expository Essay with oral presentation with visual slides, and additional related written and/or multimedia project(s)	Students will produce a research project that includes an expository analysis report, an oral presentation, and additional related written and/or multimedia project(s) *12.15 (A)* *12.20 (A–E)* *12.25 (A)*	5–7 pages typed not including bibliography, coversheet, and any graphic support **12.23 (E)** 4–5 minute oral presentation *12.25 (A)*	7 or more Aldine district resources Internet resources (reliable) LMC reference materials *12.21 (B–C)* *12.22 (B)* *8.23 (D)*	Primary and Secondary

- **Integrate writing requirements with research products**

High School Language Arts_Revised_Summer 2013

Figure 5.4. Continuum of Research Skills, Grades 11–12

Focus and Coherence	Development of Ideas (Research Conventions)	Style	Conventions	Process
Write a multi-paragraph expository essay *11.15 (A)* Effective introductions and conclusions *11.15 (Ai)* A thesis *11.23 (B); 11.15 (Aiii)* Appropriate organizing structures *11.15 (Aiv)* Logical transitions *11.15 (Aii)* Evidence and details *11.15 (A) (v)* Multiple relevant perspectives **11.15 (A) (vi)** Synthesized from several sources *11.23*	Integrate quotations and citations into written text *11.21 (C)* Organize ideas *11.21 (B)* Paraphrasing and Summarizing *11.21 (C)* Synthesize/analyze information *11.23 (A–C)* Relevant information/details *11.15 (Av)* Document with in-text citations *11.21 (C); 9.23 (D)*	Write a variety of complete sentences (i e., simple, compound, complex, compound-complex) *11.17 (A–B)*	Use standard spelling, capitalization, and punctuation *11.18 (A); 11.19 (A)—includes all TEKS in strand*	Writing Process (Pre-writing, drafting, revision, editing, conferencing, publishing) *11.13 (A–E)* Source and note cards *11.21 (C); 11.23 (D)* Research Plan *11.20 (A, B); 11.21 (A); 11.22 (A, C)* Research Vocabulary: • works cited • citation • source • synthesize • relevance • paraphrase • plagiarism • valid • MLA
Write a multi-paragraph expository essay *12.15 (A)* Effective introductions and conclusions *12.15 (Ai)* A thesis *12.23 (B); 12.15 (Aiii)* Appropriate organizing structures *12.15 (Aiv)* Logical transitions *12.15 (Aii)* Evidence and details *12.15 (A) (v)* Multiple relevant perspectives **12.15 (A) (vi)** Synthesized from several sources *12.23*	Integrate quotations and citations into written text *12.21 (C)* Organize ideas *12.21 (B)* Paraphrasing and Summarizing *12.21 (C)* Synthesize/analyze information *12.23 (A–C)* Relevant information/details *12.15 (Av)* Document with in-text citations *12.21 (C); 9.23 (D)*	Write a variety of complete sentences (i.e., simple, compound, complex, compound-complex) *12.17 (A–B)*	Use standard spelling, capitalization, and punctuation *12.18 (A); 12.19 (A)—includes all TEKS in strand*	Writing Process (Pre-writing, drafting, revision, editing, conferencing, publishing *12.13 (A–E)* Source and note cards *12.21 (C); 12.23 (D)* Research Plan *12.20 (A, B); 12.21 (A); 12.22 (A, C);* Research Vocabulary: • works cited • citation • source • synthesize • relevance • paraphrase • plagiarism • validity • reliability • MLA

We applaud this vision. To move research from a one-time (often dreaded) event to a year-long integrated adventure of inquiry speaks to the vision of leadership. As we have said, inquiry needs to be part of every writing, every genre. Aldine ISD has found a way to make it so. Aldine and Bailey have made a significant contribution to inquiry.

A NEW FORM: A NEW NAME

"There seems to be a universal and deep-rooted drive to give individual names to things. People, places, pets, and houses are among the most obvious categories, but anything with which we have a special relationship is likely to be named" (Crystal, 140). A discussion of form and genre belongs in a book (or several) by itself. For our purposes here, we want to simply touch upon the major forms as examples of how they were named.

Story

Story, Kendall Haven tells us, has been a part of human history for some 100,000 years (3). Gottschall explains, "The human mind was shaped *for* story, so that it could be shaped *by* story" (56). That, too, seems to be a deep-root drive. First came the form and then the naming of the form. The ancient Greeks called the telling of these real or fictional accounts *iotopia;* in Latin they were called *historia,* the Anglo-Normans used the word *estorie.* In fact, sometime during the Middle Ages, academia split *historia* and *estorie* into two genres: nonfiction and fiction. History became the telling of true events (his story) whereas story became the telling of pretend or made-up events.

Haven presents data that supports this binary theory, "humans intellectually set up a paradigm of binary opposites to understand new terms" (15). Hence, we have fiction and nonfiction. Hence, we have Janet Emig suggesting to Sharon Crowley that these binaries are now "straw binaries" (51).

The Novel and Novella

We named the novel the novel sometime in the 1600s because it was a new form, an elongation of story with new elements, more of everything, until it became its own form—sequenced, complex, and complicated. But the novella (from the Italian) was a "little" novel—longer than a short story but shorter than a novel.

The Essay

Our research into the essay led us to an intriguing tome *The Lost Origins of the Essay,* edited and introduced by John D'Agata. While the canon credits Montaigne as the originator of the essay, D'Agata stuns us by giving the Sumerians that honor. After the flooding of the Tigris and Euphrates river system destroyed Sumer, one lone survivor—Ziusudra—wrote a letter, a list of do's and don't's for whomever found the letter "five thousand years old—half a millennium older than the earliest known poem, a full millennium older than the earliest known story" (4). D'Agata claims this is why scholars hold that Ziusudra started literature, but D'Agata contends, "Ziusudra did something much more important. I think his list is the beginning of an alternative to nonfiction, the beginning of a form that's not propelled by information, but one compelled instead by individual expression—by *inquiry* (italics ours), by opinion, by wonder, by doubt. Ziusudra's list is the first essay in the world: it's a mind's inquisitive ramble through a place wiped clean of answers. It is trying to make a new shape where there previously was none" (4).

Next D'Agata reminds us that once people thought writing "would be a passing fad. The problem with writing, they said, is that you cannot ask it questions. When you try, it repeats itself. There is no give-and-take, no difference in what it says" (9). Then D'Agata says something so wondrous it quite literally took our breath away—so wondrous because his statement fits perfectly into our thoughts on inquiry, our stand on the critical writer. He says, "But I think the essay is an antidote to the stagnancy of writing because the essay tries to replicate the activity of the mind" (9). Inquiry. Pure inquiry. The activity of the mind.

He elaborates further, "the essay is the equivalent of the mind in rumination, performing as if improvisationally the reception of new ideas, the discovery of unknowns, the encounter with the 'other'" (9). Inquiry. Pure inquiry. The activity of the mind. The Carroll/Wilson Schemata.

Giving Susan Sontag's "Unguided Tour," where she holds a conversation with herself about herself as one example and Emerson's penchant for quoting other authors, which D'Agata identifies as "a technique that he employs not to support his working thesis but rather to introduce a new challenge to his claims" (9). As another example, his third example comes from Thucydides, who did not begin composing *The Peloponnesian War* until he had fought on both sides. This gives rise to the word *dialogue—dia—across/logos—to think*. All this D'Agata offers as foundational to make this case: " . . . 'to think through,' 'to investigate,' 'to wander.' I think that this is an inherently human activity. And I think that when we're essaying we are in a dialogue with the world" (9). Again—inquiry, pure inquiry.

So now, as we move to the French author Michel Eyquem de Montaigne (1533–1592), we note that he re-created a new literary genre, the essay, in which he used self-portrayal as a mirror of humanity. Naming his experimental form, he chose the Middle French word *essais,* which quite literally means "attempts." Eschewing the ornate and pretentious writing of the time, Montaigne literally attempted a personal style—"my simple, natural, everyday fashion, without artifice." So the father of the modern essay authentically assayed, truly attempted a new form as a response to his world and to the writing around him—a new form to examine, evaluate, experiment, and provide a provisional movement in writing—the essay—the attempt—by tentatively analyzing and describing one finite and imperfect person—himself.

Quantum leaping to Tom Romano who named collections of related types of literature *multigenre.* While Ken Macrorie, who wanted to re-emphasize what he thought we were losing in inquiry writing—the "I"—dubbed his idea the "I-Search."

Simultaneously, as Romano wrote the theory behind his notion of multigenre, Kamau Brathwaite and others were literally writing multigenre works. *Trench Town Rock* by Brathwaite and quoted in D'Agata's book deals with the violence in Kingston, Jamaica, in the early 1990s:

One report in *Trench Town Rock* is of children found dead in their home; one stabbed 70 and the other over 100 times. This engenders the Jamaica of these pages and of our times where "burning and looting" are Bob Marley song lyrics because they are normative activities in this Caribbean locale. As always with Brathwaite, part of the thrill of this book is how he visualizes these heinous experiences through font and text. Using his trademark Sycorax video-print style, each page is laid out with dramatic shifts in font-size, typography and pictograph. Each break, each slippage-in-size enacts." (Recovered by Susan Scarlata)

In today's world things change rapidly. We no longer want to wait several centuries for the concept of "essay" to take hold or be patted smooth, nor do we want to wait decades for schools to embrace "multigenre" papers in lieu of THE RESEARCH PAPER. We can't. The world is moving too fast; technology demands change. Students demand change. Since Macrorie, since Romano, we have added layers of possibilities to inquiry and tomorrow there will be more.

Shields, who has also written a unique form, which he calls "A Manifesto," peppered it with quotations, commentary, narrative, descriptions of art, exposition, references to film, film makers, philosophers, newscasters, snippets from literature and history, personal reflections, and his new form cries out for a new name. His chapters contain no titles, only numbers written on the side of the pages—some as short as a sentence, none longer than a paragraph. He uses words such as collage, montage, nonlinear, discontinuous, collage-like, an assemblage—we hear sounds "tick tick . . ." He intrigues us with references to TV shows juxtaposed with classic and sometimes little known literature. In a word—All.

Open *The Lifespan of a Fact*. Centered on the page is an excerpt from an article. Dialogue surrounds the excerpt—dialogue among the editor, the author, and the fact-checker. Certainly not the usual format for an essay. The word fiction is derived from the Latin *fictio,* which itself means "to form, to shape, to arrange"—a pretty fundamental activity in art. So D'Agata and Fingal seem to be in the business of creating a new form via arrangement. Here we are reminded of something Corita Kent believed, "Never think of a source as being static. Look at changes in the source itself " (61).

We think the new form is here, characterized paradoxically by brevity and immediacy, this new form mosaics meaning by building relationships. It layers meaning like so many sheets of transparencies one atop the other. As we see one, we get meaning, but when another is placed on top of it, the meaning changes and so it continues throughout all the layers. Andy Warhol's Campbell's Soup Can

Series lines up the iconic soup can until when we view the last can, it means something different than when we viewed the first can. Seeing all those cans in between changes our perception.

Totus

Which brings us to the question: Does art imitate life or does life imitate art? This chicken and egg conundrum may never be answered—but we know "After Freud, after Einstein, the novel retreated from narrative, poetry retreated from rhyme, and art retreated from the representational into the abstract" (Shields, 19). We always say, "We no longer live in a rhyming world," when we teach poetry. We always say, "We no longer live in an A always has a B" world when we teach outlining. While "collage, the art of reassembling fragments of preexisting images in such a way as to form a new image, was the most important innovation in the art of the twentieth century" (Shields, 19), and so collage imitated the fragmentation of the 20th century, we think we have gone beyond the I-Search, beyond multigenre, beyond collage to what we are calling "totus," the synthesizing and bringing together of parts, fragments, bits and pieces of life to create new relationships, new meanings. We think totus is the art of the 21st century.

Thus we have named the new form by using the Latin *totus*, which means whole, entire, complete, all, every part. More importantly, "totus" also means all together, all at once. A perfect word for simultaneous literacy, a perfect word for compositions (themselves a composite or a combining) of multigenres, multimodes, multimedia, a perfect word for future compositions that will envelope new technologies and technologies yet to be invented and incorporated into our canon—TOTUS—the form of the future.

Totus in Action

We advise teachers all the time to model, model, model. How else will students know the expectations? To that end, we offer a model of totus along with the caveat that while this model incorporates several genres and various media, totus is an open, flexible concept. What genre and media are chosen depends upon the purpose of the inquiry. But always totus goes through the Carroll/Wilson Schemata.

A team of two boys and two girls serve as exemplar of totus. They accessed YouTube, documentary films, Mozart's *Requiem* on CD, and recorded interviews. They incorporated the concept of Shakespearian tragedy with historical records, poetry, novels, biographies, film reviews, fiction and nonfiction, children's, YA, and MA books—even some Norse mythology. They wrote their outline and the expository introductory sections for each ACT. Further, they scripted lines, and created a totally original poem for four voices based on a mentor poem.

Matt, Sam, Brittany, and Juventina focused their inquiry on the Holocaust. Now in high school, they wanted to dig deeper into the topic they found so fascinating in middle school. And dig they did.

While space does not permit every detail of their semester quest, an outline will demonstrate the power of totus in allowing students to explore and invest in whatever genres or media fits the purpose of their inquiry.

These four decided that since the Holocaust was a tragedy on a global scale, and since it took the theme "man's inhumanity to man" to the extreme, they framed their presentation in five acts. "We used Shakespeare's tragedies as our model," they told me.

Following are their five acts:

ACT I   What Came Before the Carnage
ACT II   Yellow Stars and Blue Numbers
ACT III   Internment
ACT IV   The Final Days
ACT V   Scars but Hope

Act I: What Came Before the Carnage

Leni Riefenstahl was perhaps the biggest propagandist for Adolph Hitler. The foursome began by showing the first scenes of her powerful film *Triumph of the Will* (1935), which chronicles the 1934 Nazi Party Congress in Nuremberg. It opens with an almost mythological sequence as Hitler's airplane flies through the clouds (Valhalla?), then over the German countryside to finally land in Nuremberg among cheering people. The team explained how this film emboldened the German people and broke the backs of each country as it was shown before each Nazi invasion. Here they used YouTube. Periodically throughout the remainder of their presentation, they showed clips from this film, e.g. Hitler's bombastic speeches.

http://www.youtube.com/watch?v=GHs2coAzLJ8

Act II: Yellow Stars and Blue Numbers

This act began with a short introduction to "Kristallnacht." Then the foursome read by turn "The White Rose: Sophie Scholl (1921–1943)" from *The Music of What Happens: Poems That Tell Stories* selected by Paul B. Janeczko with Mozart's *Requiem* playing on a CD as background music.

They divided the class into two groups—those deemed "Aryan"—and those who were destined for concentration camps—the "non-Aryans." The latter group was forced to wear badges of large yellow Stars of David made out of yellow felt. Matt, Sam, Brittany, and Juventina chose the star with "Jude" imprinted in the middle because they thought it "the most dramatic." Further, these "non-Aryans" were made to stand in a line as the team marked (washable) blue numbers on their arms. The team ended ACT II by ostracizing the "non-Aryans" from the class and sending them into a "ghetto." The effect was electric. Here their inquiry had led them to the Jewish Virtual Library, www.jewishvirtuallibrary.org/jsource/Holocaust/badges.html.

Act III: Internment

Although made in 1955, Alain Resnais's film *Night and Fog,* a short 31-minute black and white documentary, shows in graphic detail man's violence toward man through old found footage and scenes of the abandoned camps of Auschwitz and Majdanek. The class was visibly shaken after viewing it. The presenters coupled this viewing with a classic film review by Peter Cowie, a noted film critic entitled "Night and Fog: Origins and Controversy." http://www.criterion.com/current/posts/289-night-and-fog-origins-and-controversy.

Act IV: The Final Days

The presenters brought in text sets of books dealing with the Holocaust. They explained they wanted to expose the class to the wealth of information available. To that end, they conducted a "Book Pass," a strategy we taught teachers adapted from *Tools for Teaching Content Literacy* by Janet Allen.

Following is a partial list of the books the students chose:

> Adler, David A. *Hilde and Eli, Children of the Holocaust.* New York: Holiday House, 1994.
>
> Adler, David A. *A Picture Book of Anne Frank.* New York: Holiday House, 1993.
>
> Auerbacher, Inge. *I Am a Star: Child of the Holocaust.* New York: Prentice-Hall Books for Young Readers, 1986.
>
> Bunting, Eve. *Gleam and Glow.* New York: Harcourt, 2001. New York: Orchard Books, 1991.
>
> Colbert, David. *10 Days Anne Frank.* New York: Aladdin Paperbacks, 2008.
>
> Craddock, Sonia. *Sleeping Boy.* New York: Atheneum, 1999.

Greenfield, Howard. *After the Holocaust.* New York: Greenwillow Books, 2001.

Hurwitz, Johanna. *Anne Frank: Life in Hiding.* New York: The Jewish Publication Society, 1988.

Lawton, Clive A. *Auschwitz.* Massachusetts: Candlewick Press, 2002.

Nolan, Han. *If I Should Die Before I Wake.* New York: Harcourt, 1994.

Rappaport, Doreen. *Beyond Courage: The Untold Story of Jewish Resistance During the Holocaust.* Massachusetts: Candlewick Press, 2012.

Rogasky, Barbara. *Smoke and Ashes: The Story of the Holocaust.* New York: Holiday House, 1988.

Rubin, Susan Goldman and Ela Weissberger. *The Cat with the Yellow Star: Coming of Age in Terezin.* New York: Holiday House, 2006.

Smith, Frank Dabba. *My Secret Camera: Life in the Lodz Ghetto.* New York: Harcourt, 2000.

Vander Zee, Ruth. *Erika's Story.* Minnesota: Creative Editions, 2003.

The team concluded Act IV with tapes of oral histories about the Holocaust collected in 1946 by Dr. David P. Boder. http://voices.iit.edu/

Act V: Scars but Hope

As their finale, the foursome did a fabulous text rendering of *Let the Celebrations Begin!* by Margaret Wild & Julie Vivas (New York: Orchard Books, 1991). This children's book tells about the cloth toys made by the Polish women in Belsen for the first children's party held after the liberation. And although this provided a note of hope, the presenters followed their rendering with an original poem that conveyed the scars of the Holocaust's brutality. They wrote the poem using the mentor text *Joyful Noise: Poems for Two Voices* by Paul Fleishman (New York: Harper & Row, 1988). The boys took one side; the girls the other, with both sides reading some of the lines together to mesh as a musical quartet of sorts. The entire experience was truly totus and surpassed in depth and breadth any "research paper."

Recently the *Houston Chronicle* ran an article by two local superintendents. In part it read, "If we want to create a college-and career-ready culture at all levels, we must recognize the real world does not work within a multiple-choice system. Students must be able to create, innovate, and problem-solve" (Smith & Cain, B-9). Totus stands ready to meet that challenge.

CONCLUDING MUSINGS

Fans of the Möbius Loop, we've written it into reading/writing connections, used it in training, created it as a symbol, and now we find ourselves applying it to inquiry. If you just make a loop (the kind kids make for Christmas decorations) you have a circle with two sides, but if you give it one twist, you get the Möbius Loop with one side running into itself. That twist changes everything.

If you start at a point and run a marker along the middle of the paper loop, the line eventually connects! If you cut along that line, you get one big Möbius Loop with both sides flowing into each other as one side. If you start at a point and run a marker close to the edge, the line connects but if you cut along that line, you get two circles—one attached to the other like a chain.

How like inquiry is the Möbius Loop. In a never-ending loop or a loop within a loop, the questions, the investigations, the curiosities are limitless. Juxtaposing a poem like "This is a Photograph of Me" by Margaret Atwood with the Claude Monet's "Water Lilies" series changes everything. But putting that same poem next to John Stone's "Early Sunday Morning" fires anew the thinking in another direction. But if you recharge the entire assemblage by adding Shakespeare's Macbeth, superimposing an obituary of a child drowning, or arranging a line drawing of concentric circles the thinking goes into high gear, the meanings begin to fold into each other, others extend beyond anything first thought making Möbius loops within Möbius loops *ad infinitum*. Burke captured the same notion with his "Pentad," with pentads within pentads indicating boundless interpretations. An inexhaustibility of meaning remains, electrifying the text. "This means, for one thing, that learning is a dynamic process that has no discernible beginning or end" (Crowley, 10). To suggest otherwise is to cheat students of the excitement of inquiry.

Just when we thought we had finished this book—if books are ever finished—we turned to each other almost in unison and said, "We need to name this new form." So, once again, through the writing, through the inquiry came the surprise, the realization. This book stands as testimony to what it says—totus.

The twists of thought and the connections are endless. When inquiry happens in that way in classrooms, follow Emerson's advice, "Place yourself in the middle of the stream of power and wisdom which animates all whom it floats, and you are without effort impelled to truth, to right and a perfect contentment."

APPENDIX

I

TEACHING THE THESIS

BY JOYCE ARMSTRONG CARROLL

Writing a good thesis provides a successful foundation for composing an essay. Teaching how to do that, how ever, is quite another matter. Teachers often say to students, "Find a thesis," or "Get a thesis," or "Bring in a thesis statement tomorrow," as if students could order one like a pizza, command it like a pet pooch, or grasp one out of thin air like a magician. Finding the genesis for a thesis is another article—this article only considers how to write one.

IDENTIFY AND DEFINE THE TERM

Students often exhibit confusion about the term "thesis." This is understandable since some teachers call it the controlling idea, central idea, main idea, proposition, claim, declaration; others label

Originally published in *School Library Monthly*, vol. 29, no. 2, November 2012, pp. 18–20. Reprinted with permission.

it the assumption, hypothesis, postulation, supposition, even the view. So first identify and define.

Coming from the Latin and Greek, "thesis" literally means the act of placing or laying down; it means to position, to propose, or to claim. The thesis literally "lays down" the writer's position at the outset of the paper so the reader has clear expectations about the paper's purpose. Quite simply, the thesis is the writer's promise to the reader. It focuses and controls the essay. Without a good solid thesis, any essay remains perilously close to becoming a mere jumble of random thoughts.

IMPORTANCE OF THE THESIS

Emphasizing the importance of the thesis helps students take seriously the crafting of it. The thesis is the main event around which everything revolves. It's like the vow—the promise—at a wedding. The flowers, attire, decorations, cake, rings, gifts, music, and food, while contributing to the event, are secondary, even tertiary, to the vow. The thesis solidifies the point, the pith; everything else supports it. In short, because the thesis promises, it holds the power of the pith! (And no one likes a broken promise.)

Kenneth Bruffee validates the importance of the thesis this way: "Suppose a writer was told, after he had just finished writing a paper, 'Save only one sentence—the sentence that says exactly what the paper says. Throw the rest away'" (*A Short Course in Writing* 1972, 43). That sentence would be the thesis sentence. So important is the thesis, it must be taught, modeled, studied, and practiced.

THE ABCS OF A GOOD THESIS

Before students begin grappling with thesis writing, they must understand its ABCs.

A—The thesis ASSERTS. Students need to be secure in their theses. Those who equivocate usually don't know much about the topic so they try to sound magnanimous. To be assertive, students need to get an angle on the topic, an aspect about which they feel confident. If preparing students for a test, suggest they take key words from prompts as nuggets to ease them into their CZ—their "confident zone." Juxtapose wishy-washy, waffling statements:

- Sometimes some people, but not all people, want a dog or some kind of a pet, maybe a bird.
- I don't know much about water skiing, but I think it is fun.

with examples of assertive statements:

- Pets make fine companions.
- Water skiing demands balance.

Model writing an assertive thesis. Think aloud as you work. Then ask students in small groups to write assertive statements about topics of interest. Display and discuss. Ask, "Does this writer sound secure?" "Is this thesis an assertion?

B—The thesis writer must BE AN INSIDER. Often students are asked to write their theses out of personal experiences. Red flag! When students hear the word "personal," they commence a personal narrative or a personal essay when the essay called for might be expository, persuasive, or analytic. Writing as an insider does not indicate a genre; it means choosing an angle as an expert about one particular aspect of the topic. For example, if the prompt reads, "Convince your parents that sports are safe," savvy writers choose a sport they know. One student may write about football safety helmets, another may choose soccer's goal safety, a third may select field hockey's eye goggles. Insider writing gives an essay edge because only insiders know those expert details that make an essay interesting. For example:

- Silky terriers make the best pets. (This student owns silky terriers.)
- Deep meanings reside in children's fairy tales. (This student avidly reads fairy tales.)

- Texting while driving causes accidents. (This student experienced a T-bone accident because the other driver was texting.)

Model writing a thesis statement as an insider. Share and walk students through the process. Then students generate theses statements as insiders about one particular aspect of topics they know. Encourage them to share and discuss.

C—The thesis statement must be CLEAR. Ah! Illusive clarity. What sometimes seems clear to the writer may be muddled mush to the reader. Three problems contribute to unclear theses: profundity, incomprehensibility of expression, and vagueness.

Students often try to sound profound in their theses, but profundity lies not in the thesis but in the body of the paper, in its defense or support of the thesis. This attempt at a philosophical or penetrating thesis thwarts what should be a simple, straightforward, and knowledgeable assertion.

Incomprehensibility of expression in the thesis confuses the focus of the essay. The thesis should pop and crackle with precise word choice, not ambiguity. Remember: It's a promise and no one likes an ambiguous promise.

When students don't know the topic (for no one can write what they don't know), they resort to machinations and shenanigans—such as vagueness. Typically, they write broad generalizations that promise nothing specific. Often students obfuscate with a thesaurus in one hand, pen in the other. By using "big" words, they reason, perhaps the reader won't notice the vacuum of knowledge. Two other crutches are writing heavy-handedly, employing impossibly long clauses that wind in and around more convolutions, or repeating information that either says nothing or perplexes the reader. Sometimes these theses are so empty of meaning, the student could plug in most anything in "support." But neophyte writers most commonly fall back on the ploy that attempts to disguise lack of knowing with pretend scholarship. "This is the unkindest cut of all," Shakespeare says, because it insults the reader. Better to be authentically simple than pretentiously erudite.

Model writing clear theses. Talk about the process. Then invite students to try their hand at writing a clear thesis—one that is simple and straightforward. Share. Discuss what makes this difficult and what makes it easy.

THE TEN CRITERIA FOR A GOOD THESIS STATEMENT

(The examples below were taken from *The New York Times Book Reviews* from March 18, March 25, and April 1, 2012. Many were altered to make the point.)

1. **Expresses the point of the paper**

   Example: *The Land of Decoration* grabbed me by the throat.
   Explanation: This thesis asserts. The writer obviously read the book and clearly states what the review will explain.

2. **Defensibility**

   Example: Technology offers an optimistic take on the future.
   Explanation: The author promises to defend positive evidence for the future of technology.

3. **Specificity**

   Example: Peter Behrens's novel *The O'Briens* follows the generations of an Irish family.
   Explanation: This thesis gives the specificity of author and title with a clear statement that the book chronicles the lives of a family through time.

4. **Conciseness**

   Example: Seventeen years ago, one terrible night changed everything.
   Explanation: The thesis presents a concise invitation to read on to discover the events of that "one terrible night" and how it "changed everything."

5. **Contains strong verbs whenever possible**

   Example: Marina Warner pursues the enigmas of imaginative desire in "The Arabian Nights."
   Explanation: "Pursues" exudes power. Students should avoid "to be" verbs if possible and choose active, dynamic verbs. (This is a teachable moment for a lesson on verb choice.)

> Working with real students tells the tale. The following email confirms the validity of this process. This comes from Yvonne Janik of Highland Park Middle School, Dallas, Texas (April 4, 2012):
>
> *Hi, Joyce,*
>
> *I have been using your ideas for thesis writing with my students these past few days, and they have been able to write correct thesis statements so much better and more quickly than in all my years of teaching thesis writing. WOW!*
>
> *THANKS!*
> *Yvonne*

6. Makes a statement—a declarative sentence

Example: Repression comes at a high price.

Explanation: Specific, concise, straightforward, assertive and confident, this thesis promises an insider's explanation of "repression" and what the author means by "a high price."

7. Avoids bifurcation

Example: John Leonard championed women authors and writers of color.

Explanation: Bifurcation (students love the word and remember it because it sounds naughty) calls upon the author to defend, explain, or analyze two things: how Leonard championed "women authors" and then how he championed "writers of color." Better, especially on tests, to take on one aspect—not two or three.

8. Does not give away the strategy

Example: A psychologist argues that people base decisions on moral intuition, not reason.

Explanation: Two problems occur here. The strategy of arguing is given. This is tantamount to the student saying, "I am going to persuade in favor of . . ." or "I am going to tell you about. . . ." Rather, the strategy should become clear in the body of the essay. Second, a problem with bifurcation—what people base decisions upon and what they do not base decisions upon—could easily muddle a paper. Stick to one aspect.

9. **Shuns excessive wordiness**

Example: Cristina Garcia's fiction—from her first novel *Dreaming in Cuban* through her fifth *The Lady Matador's Hotel*—is known for traversing continents, cultures, and generations, and for telling the stories of families, friends, and strangers thrown together and torn apart in uncertain times.

Explanation: Most of what this thesis promises belongs in the body of the paper. A more concise thesis would be: Cristina Garcia's fiction tells the stories of families. Then in the exposition or analysis, the writer takes on "traversing continents, cultures, and generations" in several paragraphs, "friends and strangers" in a paragraph or two, and concludes with how all this is "thrown together and torn apart in uncertain times." (This common mistake of students leaves them in a quandary about what to write when they get to the body of the paper because they feel they have already written it.)

10. **Never asks a question**

Example: What do philosophy and religion reveal about life?

Explanation: A thesis statement calls for a declaration, not an interrogation. Crafting the thesis as a question seems weaker, as if the writer can't quite get started, isn't confident, or vainly attempts to appeal to the reader. State the thesis confidently and then go forth to explain, persuade, or analyze.

In order to craft a sound thesis, students need exposure to these criteria (characteristics) of a good thesis. They need to:

- learn the criteria,
- see a model of how to analyze a couple of theses using that criteria,
- analyze theses independently through mentor texts, giving a thumbs-up for those that meet the criteria and revising those that don't,
- practice revising theses using that criteria, and
- practice writing theses statements.

APPENDIX

III

FINDING THE GENESIS FOR A THESIS

BY JOYCE ARMSTRONG CARROLL

Perhaps in all of "writing-dom," generating a thesis or digging into the origin of a subject worthy of a thesis rises up as the most difficult. Born out of Aristotle's notion of invention, contemporary rhetoricians, using the educational jargon of the day, dub this part of the writing process "prewriting." Actively systematic or subconsciously random, this search for subject finds students mentally (with or without pen in hand) thrashing around in their efforts to find or to focus an idea—sometimes nebulous, usually fragile, always ephemeral—for their papers.

Teachers try to help this seeking by providing strategies—freewriting, brainstorming, listing, journals, dialectical notebooks, even doodling or drawing, among others—to hasten the search. Sometimes these strategies yield great success, but just as often they lead to abysmal failure.

Originally published in *School Library Monthly*, vol. 29, no. 6, March 2013, pp. 17–19. Reprinted with permission.

A STRATEGY THAT WORKS

I submit a prewriting strategy—based on heuristics—that works. The word "heuristics" comes from the Greek *heuriskein*, "to discover," and reaches us over the centuries as a procedure or a guide in solving a problem. Popularized in the 1960s, heuristics as a taxonomy of sorts won favor as a logical, but not formulaic, strategy that nudged students to consider multiple possibilities, break out of writing ruts, and create new connections that trigger new understandings. Thus, heuristics move thinking and writing from the simple to the complex (and perhaps back again in its recursive journey) to help nail concepts or, in this case, ideas. Hence, when students use this strategy, they more likely find the genesis of their thesis. Then it is just a matter of honing it according to the criteria of a good thesis (see *SLM*, November 2012, pages 18–20). Young, Becker, and Pike describe the three functions of the heuristic procedure:

- It aids in retrieving relevant information stored in the mind.
- It draws attention to important information that can be further researched or accessed.
- It prepares the mind for the intuition of an ordering principle or hypothesis (1970, 120).

(For an in-depth look at the scholarship behind heuristics, see: Lauer, Janice M. *Invention in Rhetoric and Composition*. Parlor Press LLC, 2004.)

THE HEURISTIC TOPIC: TOPICS, THEMES, WTS

Deceptively simple, this particular heuristic, which I call "Topics, Themes, WTS (Working Thesis Statement)," jibes with Donald M. Murray's contention that once students discover that the strength of their writing depends directly on the vigor of their thinking, they become "see-ers" (1968, 2). In essence these students perceive their world through the lens of possibilities. Therefore, Topics, Themes, WTS metaphorically takes the student's mind by the hand and leads that mind from myriad possibilities to framing a well-considered thesis.

THE PROCEDURE

Topics

Students fold an 8 ½ × 11 sheet of paper into thirds, creating a horizontal tri-fold (a "burrito" fold). If folding paper doesn't hold any appeal, students may just divide a paper into three columns. At the top of column one, extreme left, students write "TOPICS."

Teachers can help students realize that topics are one- or two-word connections related to their assignment or to the prompt if they are in a testing situation. For example: If they are writing a paper on *Charlotte's Web* by E.B. White, they may list farm, spider, pigs, death, a plan, hope, friends, and so forth. For *Lilly's Purple Plastic Purse* by Kevin Henkes they may list school, teachers, disobedience, anger, understanding. For *Beowulf*, students may list hero, villain, kennings, Anglo-Saxons, ogres, kings, England, legends. If they are responding to a prompt on a test such as "Write an essay explaining why you want to play a sport in school," they may list friends, makes muscles, builds character, fun, exercise, more practice, school spirit, soccer, basketball, volleyball.

Because this first step in the heuristic strikes students as easy and non-threatening (although, in truth, this mind tapping is indeed higher-level thinking), they, with little effort, generate a series of topics associated with the assignment or the prompt. In turn, these topics provide the cognitive springboard for themes.

Themes

Before students generate their themes, use this perfect teachable moment for teaching theme. Begin by playing Rimsky-Korsakov's *Scheherazade*. Even younger children understand the grim music that matches the cruel Sultan Schariar. After his introduction, though, the music changes for the leitmotif that represents the storyteller Scheherazade. Both sweet and tender, this unison musical phrase plays, albeit with different instruments, each time she begins to tell a new story. This device, *leitmotif*, unifies the piece. From "Sinbad the Sailor" to the "Festival at Baghdad," Scheherazade tells through music some of the stories of The Arabian Nights. Much like the *leitmotif* in music, themes in writing are the "melodies" that weave the central idea throughout the entire piece.

In good literature and in good writing, themes are generally universal. William Faulkner, in his acceptance speech for the Nobel Prize, gave us a listing of these "old verities and truths of the heart, the old universal truths . . . love and honor and pity and pride and compassion and sacrifice" (Faulkner 1950). Sharing stories and poems with these themes crystallizes the concept for students. At this point, students label column two, the middle column, "THEMES."

Themes build upon topics but are usually expressed in phrases, clauses, or sentences (this is a good time to review those grammatical concepts). A theme embeds the message throughout a piece of writing. Rarely does a piece of literature contain only one theme—usually there are many, therefore, they are labeled in the field as "major" and "minor"—but always one theme predominates. So for the students, the act of discovery continues.

Charlotte's Web may yield "even animals face death," "it's good to have a plan," "hope keeps us going," "friends are essential." For *Lilly*, themes may be "there's a time and place for everything," "good teachers understand kids." For *Beowulf*, "the eternal battle between good and evil," "the ogre Grendel symbolizes evil / Beowulf symbolizes good," "heroes never give up." Themes growing out of the topics related to the test prompt may be "sports promote character," "engaging in sports shows school spirit".

Using this heuristic strategy enables a more sustained understanding of theme as students ruminate on the topics, think more deeply about them, and have time to allow their brains to range over the ideas they generate. This movement from topics to themes is also a movement from one level of thinking to a deeper, higher level. Coming up with the theme "little kids are egocentric" takes deeper cognition than the topic "little kids."

WTS—Working Thesis Statement

Because of all the thinking and writing evidenced in the columns of the tri-fold tool, coming up with a subject and honing that subject becomes an easier task. Given the criteria of a good thesis statement, students begin the mental work of considering their topics and themes as they construct a working thesis statement, or central or controlling idea. (These terms are synonymous, often used interchangeably or with different grade levels.) Calling it a working thesis statement allows students wiggle room to revise and refine their subject as they write their way through the paper.

A working thesis for *Charlotte's Web* may read "Friends give us hope." This WTS allows the writer to explain how friends provide hope in our lives. Using Charlotte and Wilbur as examples, this working thesis supplies the necessary underpinnings for a good expository essay. This thesis exhibits conciseness and preciseness. Clearly, the major words "friends" and "hope" will be defined, then explained through examples both personal and in the book itself.

For *Lilly*, a working thesis might be "Success depends upon good timing," which builds upon Lilly's penchant for immediacy. This working central idea could lead directly to a personal narrative—a story where the major character achieves a goal through good timing. *Lilly's Purple Plastic Purse* could be used as an example, the character could be reading the book, or a reference to the book could be used as a zippy conclusion. This focus will serve the writer well. Keeping that working idea in mind throughout the writing of the story, the student can capitalize on a very basic tenant of storytelling—timing.

"The epic Beowulf delivers our first action hero" stands as a solid working thesis begging for a persuasive essay. The author may offer evidence to convince the reader of its validity by using Beowulf as the archetypal character who prefigures the action heroes in literature, film, and video today. Specificity empowers this thesis.

The author of this WTS, though, could just as easily use this thesis for an analytical paper. Students analyze the action parts of the epic: the scene where Beowulf's iron grip on Grendel's arm causes the ogre to tear himself free and run one-armed into the night, or Beowulf's fight with Grendel's mother. Another avenue for analysis may be quoting lines that prove Beowulf's uncommon prowess, "he now has the strength of thirty men." With both approaches, the student works through Beowulf's adventures connecting them to present-day action figures and thus supports the WTS.

For the test prompt, the WTS may be: "Sports build character." Here the WTS sets up a cause/effect expository essay as its organizational structure. Given the time constraints in testing situations, this WTS helps the writer by providing the foundational architecture for the delivery system of cause (sports) and effect (building character). The writer may then flesh out a specific sport and show, for example, how playing that sport fosters the integrity of being true to self while sensitive to the team or even to the competition.

IN SUMMARY

Writing a good paper comes down to this: reception and perception. Rimsky-Korsakov used the same notes as other composers, but he put them together in new and different ways. Students use the same words as other writers, but when they have that thesis statement down pat, when it focuses their view, their words will follow that thread into a coherent, unified whole composition. Clearly, when students literally have the tools of the thesis criteria coupled with a handy heuristic at their fingertips, they will do better on writing assignments. The effective use of the heuristic strategy in finding the genesis for a thesis can be summed up this way: Topics, Themes, WTS allows for connections between what is taught and what is thought.

REFERENCES

Murray, Donald M. *A Writer Teaches Writing*. Houghton Mifflin, 1968.

William Faulkner on the Web. "William Faulkner's Nobel Prize Speech." 1950. http://www.mcsr.olemiss.edu/~egjbp/faulkner/lib_nobel.html (accessed December 7, 2012).

Young, Richard E., Alton L. Becker, and Kenneth L. Pike. *Rhetoric: Discovery and Change*. Harcourt, Brace & World, Inc., 1970.

APPENDIX III

THE DOCUMENTED ESSAY

BY JOYCE ARMSTRONG CARROLL

Change is everywhere; it's in the air—corporations no longer require business suits, restaurants have gone casual, even church services have relaxed. While my alma mater grapples with decisions revolving around graduate classes and how to preserve the pristine estate of George Jay Gould at Georgian Court University, Burka asks about Texas A&M, "Can the forces of change overcome the forces of resistance?" ("Corps Values," *Texas Monthly*, May 2004).

Ah! A noble question. A question worthy of some high school teachers and college professors who remain wedded to the fifteen-page research paper, requiring note cards—fifty for an A (do they really not know about photocopy machines?)—endnotes (or even footnotes) on quaint topics easily accessible (plagiarized?) from the Internet. Their resistance, often offered in the name of scholarship, is not only outdated but also downright antediluvian.

Reprinted by permission from: *R&E Journal*. "From the Director's: The Documented Essay." Spring/Summer 2004, Spring, TX: New Jersey Writing Project in Texas, vol. xii, no. 1, pp. 10–11.

The much-quoted Marcus Aurelius Antoninus (121–180) cautioned in his *Meditations III,* "Everything is in a state of metamorphosis. Thou thyself art in everlasting change" (translated by Gregory Hayes, Oxford University Press, 1998). But some hold onto that research paper!

So I got to thinking. Perhaps they are unfamiliar with the documented essay, research writing that includes a limited number of research sources, providing full documentation parenthetically within the text. This form works well and invites students not to put all their eggs in one research basket, but to illuminate what they know about subjects in shorter pieces with more teeth.

How grand to invite one documented essay that includes a survey or an interview; another with research out of journals, newspapers, and magazines; a third with sources from the Internet; a fourth with books as the documentation; a fifth with a touch of TV, other media, or a combination of sources. How quickly the teacher could assess, refine, correct, and hone the research capabilities of students—immediately, not at the end of a semester when the students, with great heaves and sighs, turn in the dreaded paper knowing they will pass or fail but in either case move on.

All of which reminds me that in October 1985, I wrote an article titled "TV and Term Papers," published in *English Journal.* Way before state-mandated tests contained open-ended items that invited connections, I began with a quote from Wilfred Trotter, "Knowledge comes from noticing resemblances and recurrences in the events that happen around us." I invited teachers to consider the times and programs such as *20/20, The Today Show, Good Morning America,* or *60 Minutes* which tick through topics as diverse as SIDS, "The Minister of Cocaine," and a profile on Red Smith. I asked them to eschew "term paper time," and I assimilated "into the teaching of the term paper what students assimilate when watching TV shows that research, document, investigate, explore, and inquire" (85).

I used as support Janet Emig's "Hand, Eye, Brain: Some 'Basics' in the Writing Process," where she states, "the eye is probably the major sense modality for presenting experience to the brain" (Cooper and Odell, *Research on Composing,* NCTE, 1978), information most recently reinforced in Richard Restak's *The New Brain* (Rodale Books, 2003). I also tapped the work of my students—one who told about how she was accepted by Ford Modeling, another who explained how her family dealt with her brain-damaged brother. These students were doing research in every sense of the word, true research, research that captured their interest, research they owned about topics they truly wanted to know more about. Isn't that at the basis of all good writing?

Now over twenty years later, I again make a plea for the documented essay. Though it may make use of personal observations and examples, it is not a personal essay. While a documented essay may be biographical, historical, scientific, or general informational, it

- documents research and gives supporting references;
- provides information on a specific topic;
- contains references to source material *within* the text of essay;
- is shorter than a term paper (which suggests by its very name prolonged work over six or nine weeks);
- contains fewer sources;
- is clearly and effectively organized. (For a Self-Assessment Rubric for the documented essay, see *Prentice Hall Writing and Grammar: Communication in Action, Diamond Level*, p. 266.)

Students are able to efficiently write a documented essay about something that interests them, something about which they are expert. Over the years, students have written three-to five-page documented essays on high school, college, hobbies, the beauty of a foreign country, football, math class, pets, cheerleading, painting, and books. All valid essays. All documented. All pithy and interesting.

I urge teachers to validate the documented essay in class; I urge teachers to write one or more and submit to appropriate publications. I urge us all to incorporate the documented essay into many, indeed all, assignments—replacing the one "biggy" with bantam but better papers. My experience has led me to realize that when students write many essays with spurts of documentation, they actually do more research, better research, and authentic research. The by-product is that teachers then have the opportunity to catch flaws along the way—all along the way. It's a win/win situation.

(Just for the record, please note that you have just read a documented essay.)

REFERENCES

Aldine I.S.D., Texas. "Continuum of Research Skills and Requirements for Performance Based Assessment, Grades 9–10."

Aldine I.S.D., Texas. "Continuum of Research Skills and Requirements for Performance Based Assessment, Grades 11–12."

Aldine I.S.D., Texas. "Year at a Glance 2013–2014, English I."

Atwell, Nancie. *In the Middle* (2nd ed.) New Hampshire: Heinemann, 1998.

Braithwaite, Kamau. *Trench Town Rock.* Kelly, Wyoming: Lost Roads Publishing, 1994/2009 & 1993.

Bruffee, Kenneth A. *A Short Course in Writing.* Massachusetts: Winthrop, 1972.

Bunting, Eve. *Pop's Bridge.* New York: Harcourt, 2006.

Carr, Nicholas. *The Shallows: What the Internet Is Doing to Our Brains.* New York: W. W. Norton, 2010.

Carroll, Joyce Armstrong. "Finding the Genesis for a Thesis." *School Library Monthly.* Vol. 29, No. 6 (2013) 17–19.

Carroll, Joyce Armstrong. "Teaching the Thesis." *School Library Monthly.* Vol. 29, No.2 (2012) 18–20.

Carroll, Joyce Armstrong and Edward E. Wilson. *Acts of Teaching: How to Teach Writing.* Colorado: Teacher Ideas Press, 1993.

Carroll, Joyce Armstrong and Edward E. Wilson. *Acts of Teaching: How to Teach Writing: A Text, A Reader, A Narrative* (2nd ed.). California: Libraries Unlimited, 2008.

Carroll, Joyce Armstrong and Edward E. Wilson. *Poetry After Lunch: Poems to Read Aloud.* Texas: Absey & Co., 1997.

Crowley, Sharon. *A Teacher's Introduction to Deconstruction.* Illinois: NCTE, 1989.

Crystal, David. *The Cambridge Encyclopedia of the English Language.* New York: Cambridge University Press, 1995.

D'Agata, John (edited and introduced). *The Lost Origins of the Essay.* MN: Graywolf Press, 2009.

D'Agata, John and Jim Fingal. *The Lifespan of a Fact.* New York: W. W. Norton, 2012.

Eagleman, David. *Incognito: The Secret Lives of the Brain.* New York: Vintage, 2011.

Emerson, Ralph Waldo. *Spiritual Laws* (181). Maryland: ArcManor, 2007.

Emig, Janet. "Writing as a Mode of Learning," "The Uses of the Unconscious in Composing," and "Hand, Eye, Brain: Some 'Basics' in the Writing Process." *The Web of Meaning: Essays on Writing, Teaching, Learning, and Thinking* (Dixie Goswami and Maureen Butler, eds.). New York: Boynton/Cook Publishers, 1983.

Freedman, Aviva and Ian Pringle (eds.). *Reinventing the Rhetorical Tradition.* Arkansas: L & S Books, 1980.

Forester, E. M. *Aspects of the Novel.* Florida: Harcourt, 1927/1955.

Gendlin, Eugene. *Experiencing and the Creation of Meaning: A Philosophical and Psychological Approach to the Subjective.* Illinois: Northwestern University Press, 1997.

Gendlin, Eugene. *Focusing.* New York: Bantam Books, 2007.

Gottschall, Jonathan. *The Storytelling Animal: How Stories Make Us Human.* New York: Houghton Mifflin Harcourt, 2012.

Haven, Kendall. *Story Proof: The Science Behind the Startling Power of Story.* Connecticut: Libraries Unlimited, 2007.

Healy, Jane M. *Endangered Minds: Why Our Children Don't Think.* New York: Simon & Schuster, 1990.

Hylton, Wil S. "Lights, Action: The Alternate Realities of James Turrell," *The New York Times Magazine,* June 16, 2013, 34–41 & 58–59.

Ingham, Zita. *Reading and Writing a Landscape: A Rhetoric of Southwest Desert Literature.* Arizona: The University of Arizona, 1991.

Keene, Ellin Oliver. *To Understand: New Horizons in Reading Comprehension.* New Hampshire: Heinemann, 2008.

Kent, Corita and Jan Steward. *Learning by Heart: Teachings to Free the Creative Spirit.* New York: Allworth Press, 2008.

Kuhlthau, Carol C., Leslie K. Maniotes, and Ann K. Caspari. *Guided Inquiry: Learning in the 21st Century.* Connecticut: Libraries Unlimited, 2007.

Lauer, Janice M. *Invention in Rhetoric and Composition.* Indiana: Parlor Press, 2004.

Macrorie, Ken. *Searching Writing.* New Jersey: Hayden Book Co., 1980.

McLuhan, Marshall. *Understanding Media: The Extensions of Man.* California: Gingko, 2003.

Murray, Donald M. "Teaching the Other Self: The Writer's First Reader." *College Composition and Communication.* Vol. 33, No. 2 (May 1982) 140–147.

Murray, Donald M. "A Writer Teaches Writing: A Practical Method of Teaching." *The Essential Don Murray: Lessons from America's Greatest Writing Teacher* (Thomas Newkirk and Lisa C. Miller, eds.). New Hampshire: Boynton/Cook, 2009.

Ondaatje, Michael. *The Collected Works of Billy the Kid.* New York: Vintage, 1970/2008.

Perl, Sondra. *Felt Sense: Writing with the Body.* New Hampshire: Boynton/Cook, 2004.

Perl, Sondra and Arthur Egendorf. "The Process of Creative Discovery: Theory, Research, and Implications for Teaching." *The Territory of Language* (Donald A. McQuade, ed.). Illinois: Southern Illinois University Press, 1986.

Polanyi, Michael. *Personal Knowledge: Towards a Post-Critical Philosophy.* Illinois: The University of Chicago Press, 1962.

Ramachandran, V. S. and Diane Rogers-Ramachandran. "Mind the Gap." *Scientific American Digital*, Vol. 18, No. 2 (2008) 4–7.

Romano, Tom. *Blending Genre, Altering Style: Writing Multigenre Papers.* New Hampshire: Boynton/Cook, 2000.

Romano, Tom. *Writing with Passion: Life Stories, Multiple Genres.* New Hampshire: Boynton/Cook, 1995.

Scarlata, Susan. "*Trench Town Rock* by Kamau Braithwaite & *Standing Wave* by John Taggart." http://www.octopusmagazine.com/Issue 14/scarlata.htm.

Schön, Donald A. *The Reflective Practitioner: How Professionals Think in Action.* New York: Basic Books, 1983.

Shields, David. *Reality Hunger: A Manifesto.* New York: Vintage Books, 2010.

Smith, Greg and Jim Cain. "Legislative Changes Bring Opportunities for Learning." *Houston Chronicle,* Sunday, August 25, 2013, B-9.

Strong, Michael. *The Habit of Thought: From Socratic Seminars to Socratic Practice.* North Carolina: New View Publications, 1997.

Reist, Melinda Tankard. "Pageants Reeking of Blatant Exploitation." *Sunday Herald-Sun* (Melbourne), July 15, 2012, 2.

Russell, Peter. *The Brain Book.* New York: Dutton, 1979.

Vygotsky, L. S. *Thought and Language.* Translated by Eugenia Hanfmann and Gertrude Vakar. Massachusetts: MIT Press, 1962.

Wrathall, Mark A. *Heidegger and Unconcealment: Truth, Language, and History.* New York: Cambridge University Press, 2011.

Young, Richard E., Alton L. Becker, and Kenneth L. Pike. *Rhetoric: Discovery and Change.* New York: Harcourt, Brace & World, 1970.

INDEX

Note: Italicized page numbers indicate a figure on the corresponding page. Page numbers followed by *t* indicate a table on the corresponding page.

ABOUT THE AUTHORS

JOYCE ARMSTRONG CARROLL, EdD, HLD is co-director of Abydos Literacy Learning. Her published works include Libraries Unlimited's *Acts of Teaching: How to Teach Writing, Brushing Up on Grammar,* and *Four by Four: Practical Methods for Writing Persuasively.* Carroll has been in the field of education for 55 years, teaching every grade level including 18 years of college teaching.

EDWARD E. WILSON is co-director of Abydos Literacy Learning. His published works include Libraries Unlimited's *Acts of Teaching: How to Teach Writing, Brushing Up on Grammar,* and *Four by Four: Practical Methods for Writing Persuasively.* Wilson owns Absey, a small publishing company that specializes in teacher idea books.